Stop Spinning Your Wheels

Using Results-Based Accountability to Steer Your Agency to Success

Stop Spinning Your Wheels
Using Results-Based Accountability to Steer Your Agency to Success

Anne McIntyre-Lahner

To order additional books go to clearimpact.com

ISBN 978-0-578-18421-0

Library of Congress Control Number: 2016910089

To my parents, who taught me the importance of contributing to my community.

To my daughters and their families - Kate, Aaron and Julianna; Liz, John, and Scout; and Olivia - they inspire me to try to make a difference.

And to my husband Mark, who is my "better off," and who always encourages me to Turn the Curve.

Table of Contents

Acknowledgements ix

Preface xi

Chapter 1: Introduction 1

Chapter 2: A Starting Place: How We Made the 11
Connecticut Kids Report Card Happen

Chapter 3: Moving Forward: Using RBA to Align 21
the Report Card and Departmental Work

Chapter 4: Implementing RBA Across the Department 25

Chapter 5: Managing Departmental Performance................36

Chapter 6: Nine Lessons Learned Along the Way 54

Chapter 7: Final Reflection 66

Appendix A: Results-Based Accountability™ 71
Terms Defined

Appendix B: Text of CT Act Requiring an Annual 76
Results-Based Accountability Report
Card Evaluating Policies and Programs
Impacting Children

Appendix C: RBA Report Card Template 79

Appendix D: PowerPoint Presentation: Hands On!..................81
Creating your RBA Report Card

Appendix E: PowerPoint Presentation: Introduction to 94
Using RBA to Strengthen Services for the
Well-being of Connecticut's Kids.

Appendix F: Governor's Cabinet on Nonprofit Health 105
and Human Services: Recommendations
of the Population Results Workgroup
(October 30, 2013).

Appendix G: Turning Curves at the Connecticut 127
Department of Children and Families

About the Author ....Back Cover

Acknowledgements

With gratitude and appreciation to my mentors and partners in the work:

For your guidance, support, and technical assistance: Mark Friedman, Phil Lee, Adam Luecking, Bennet Pudlin, Barry Goff, Janice Gruendel, Olivier Kamanda, Joette Katz, Ron Schack, Diana Urban, Kayleigh Weaver, and Michael Williams;

For initiating and continuing to support the RBA work in Connecticut: the Co-Chairs of the Connecticut General Assembly Appropriations Committee, past and present, including Representative Denise Merrill (currently Connecticut Secretary of the State), Senator Toni Harp (currently Mayor of New Haven, CT), Representative John Geragosian (currently CT State Auditor), Representative Toni Walker, and Senator Beth Bye;

For being great RBA partners: Erica Bromley, Christine Dauser, Liz Giannaros, Ajit Gopalkrishnan, Brian Hill, Jill Jensen, Susan Keane, Rick Porth, and Charlene Russell-Tucker;

For ongoing support, data development, RBA report card coaching, and contracts work that got us to where we are: Lara Beecher, David Brennan Alyssa Carboni, Yadira Ijeh, Judi Jordan, Chris Marcelli, Mike Mocadlo, Suzanne Neafus, Fred North, Steve Roe, Diane Rosell, Bekah Rupert, Ted Sanford, Susan Smith, Isabel Turmeque, and Aislinn Walsh;

For changing the way we approach our work: the DCF Program Development and Oversight Coordinators, and regional, divisional, and facility management teams;

For ongoing work to ensure Connecticut's children are better off: my colleagues at the Connecticut Department of Children and Families ("DCF") - this book is about all of us working together to ensure Connecticut's children and families are better off.

Preface

This is an inspiring book about what it takes to create change in a large government organization. It shows how the RBA concepts of population and performance accountability can put the role of the agency in perspective; and how that perspective can be used to create partnerships across the provider community and across the state. It tells the story of how such a broadly based partnership was used to create the Connecticut Kids Report Card. And it tells the continuing story of how committed leadership in the Department of Children and Families ("DCF" or the "Department") is making progress on infusing performance accountability into the culture of the organization. The book is filled with practical lessons and advice about what it takes to make changes at this scale. I have worked with Anne and her colleagues and can testify to the energy and commitment they bring to the work. If any of the challenges discussed here sound familiar, you will definitely want to read this book.

> \- Mark Friedman
> Santa Fe September 2016

Chapter 1

Introduction

"Never doubt that a small group of thoughtful, committed people can change the world. Indeed, it is the only thing that ever has." - Margaret Mead

I believe we all get into public service and non-profit work to change the world.

We start our careers with enthusiasm, ready to take on the challenges that stand in our way and in the way of those whom we want to serve. But no one walks away without confronting a few obstacles in the road.

Over time, budget cuts and evolving priorities affect our ability to make the changes we seek. Learning how to navigate those challenges can become part of the job, but they still have the power to derail good work.

Eventually, we learn that despite our efforts, we haven't solved the problems we set out to tackle. Sometimes it feels like no matter how hard we work, we don't have an impact.

I also believe that the agencies and organizations within which we work are not focused on achieving the results and outcomes we desire. They are focused on "what we do," rather than "what we can achieve." As a result, the systems and processes originally put in place to increase accountability take on a life of their own and change our focus from outcomes to outputs.

I started in the human services field, as I imagine many readers of this book did, because I wanted to make a difference. So this book is for anyone working at the local, state or national level, interested in changing agency culture to focus on outcomes, not processes.

My intent is two-fold - to explain how Results-Based Accountability™ ("RBA") can help make your work more effective, and to share some of the lessons I have learned implementing RBA in a large agency.

RBA is a management framework developed by Mark Friedman, author of *Trying Hard Is Not Good Enough*. Mark is a seasoned public administration professional with over thirty years of experience, who grew frustrated with all the time organizations spent worrying about all the "stuff" that they do rather than the outcomes they are trying to achieve.

As the Director of Performance Management for Connecticut's Department of Children and Families ("DCF"), I use RBA on a daily basis. It not only serves as the framework for developing agency strategies, but it also helps my work with DCF colleagues as they develop their regional and division-wide strategies and performance measures, and with provider partners as they develop strategies to improve performance in the services they provide for DCF.

My hope is that through reading this book, you'll anticipate what RBA can do for your organization and for your own professional development. And I am excited that you are starting your RBA journey because it will save you countless hours of unproductive time and wasted energy. It can be the difference between driving change and spinning your wheels. Because after all, what's the point of hard work if your efforts aren't working?

My Two Rules

If I had to summarize the key takeaways from implementing RBA in my agency, there would only be two rules:

Rule 1. Start with the end in mind.
Rule 2. There are no other rules.

Okay, maybe I oversimplified.

Think of it in the following way:

When you take a vacation, which of these do you think to yourself?

"I'm going to head to the airport tomorrow and see what flights are heading out of town"

or

"I'd like to take a week off somewhere warm like San Diego. I wonder how to find the best way to get there."

Most of us think in line with the second statement. We think about our destination first - where we want to be. Only then do we determine how we want to get there and what we need to do to make that happen.

It's no different with human services work. RBA reminds us that if you want to make a difference in your organization, your state government, or your agency, you first need to figure out where you want to end up. This is the result or outcome you want to achieve.

That little shift in perspective can help us set clearer sights on our desired results. And with better focus, those results become more attainable.

So let's start with the end result in mind. Take a minute to consider what inspired you to pursue human services work. What change or impact in your community do you seek? What is motivating you to take this journey? Once you've visualized why this work is important to you, you'll be ready to tackle it head on.

The Language of RBA

The RBA framework takes aim at the traditional way of doing things. Jargon goes out and plain language comes in. Using clear language that everyone can understand is a challenge. Whether our backgrounds are in child welfare, education, criminal justice or any other system, we tend to bring our own assumptions, jargon, bureaucratic speak and acronyms to conversations.

RBA's straightforward approach allows everyone to share their ideas and ask questions on equal footing. We intentionally use accessible language and write so that taxpayers, legislators, and community members can understand and participate in the process. A limited, but important set of RBA terms helps us answer the three core RBA questions:

(1) How much did we do?
(2) How well did we do it?
(3) Is anyone better off?

Before I get too far along, I'll introduce the key RBA terms now. The definitions build upon each other, so we'll start with the most fundamental concepts and move on from there.

Key Terms (in order of importance)[1]

Population Level Accountability: Population level accountability is about the well-being of whole populations. Within the RBA framework, population level work actually refers to entire populations (or subpopulations) within a geographic location, not a client population. This is different from what we usually think of as "population," in that public and private agencies usually identify their population as the clients to whom they target their services, or those they are mandated or funded to serve.

Results Statement: This describes the desired conditions of well-being for a population of children, adults, or families in a specific geographic area. Connecticut's population results statements include: healthy children; safe children; children living in stable environments; children ready for

---

1 Adopted from Connecticut General Assembly. Glossary of RBA Terms Used in Connecticut. Web. 2 February 2014 available at:
https://uatext1.cga.ct.gov/app/rba/2015/CT%20RBA%20Glossary.pdf and Mark Friedman's Results Accountability Implementation Guide, www.raguide.org/RA/the_language_of_accountability.htm

success; and strong families and safe communities. Results statements are positively worded, and are usually fairly brief and general.

Population Indicators: Indicators measure the results statement; they quantify and qualify the results with population-level data. As Mark Friedman explains, they answer the question, "How would we recognize these results in measurable terms if we fell over them?" For example, a population indicator like *crime rate* helps quantify whether we are living in *safe communities*. As with population-level results, indicators measure data for entire populations and not just client populations. We look at these data over time to see if we are making a difference, or using RBA language, to see if we are "Turning the Curve," which is described below. Sometimes indicators are categorized as "headline indicators" for those that measure the primary or most important data, and "secondary indicators" for those that measure interesting, but less critical data.

Population Level Questions - The Seven Population Accountability Questions:

1. What are the quality of life conditions we want for the children, adults and families who live in our community? (Population Results)

2. What would these conditions look like if we could see them? (Experience)

3. How can we measure these conditions? (Population Indicators)

4. How are we doing on the most important of these measures? (Baselines and Causes)

5. Who are the partners that have a role to play in doing better?

6. What works to do better, including no-cost and low-cost ideas? (Possible actions)

7. What do we propose to do? (Action Plan)

Strategies: Strategies are coherent collections of actions that have a reasoned chance of achieving results. Strategies are made up of our best thinking about what works, and they often include the contributions of many partners. Strategies can be developed at the population level and also at the performance level. And, as I'll repeat throughout this book, no single action by any agency or provider can create the improved results and outcomes we want and need.

Performance Level Accountability: Performance level accountability is about the performance of service systems, agencies and programs, and the well-being of client populations (as opposed to whole populations). Almost all of the work performed within service systems, public and private agencies, and programs is done at the performance level. This is very important to understand and is discussed further in this book.

Performance Measures: Performance measures demonstrate how well public and private agencies are working at the program level, both as individual agencies, and as a part of a "system" of services. The most important performance measures tell us whether the clients or customers of the service are better off (*Is anyone better off?* is one of the three core RBA performance questions). We sometimes refer to these measures as client or customer results (to distinguish them from population level results for all children and families). The other types of program performance measures answer the questions *How much did we do?* and *How well did we do it?*

Turning the Curve: Instead of focusing on hitting a particular benchmark or target by a certain date, RBA stresses the importance of change over time. Turning the Curve describes efforts to improve the direction or rate of change in the baseline of an indicator or performance measure. It is also shorthand for the process of determining whether the current and projected level on an indicator or performance measure is acceptable or requires change. We Turn the Curve with strategies and actions that are based on What Works: what we know from the research, best practices, and our own experience is likely to address the story behind the baselines.

Data Development Agenda: The Data Development Agenda is a prioritized list of where new or better data is needed to answer each of the three core RBA questions introduced above: (1) *How much did we do?* (2) *How well did we do it?* (3) *Is anyone better off?* Using a data development agenda allows us to acknowledge that we don't have all the information we need, but we can still move forward with the work instead of waiting to get the desired data.

Information and Research Agenda: The information and research agenda provides a disciplined way of pursuing unanswered questions that arise from the RBA process. Questions on this agenda address both causes behind the data, and what works (best practice) to Turn the Curve.

Performance Level Questions - The Seven Talk-to-Action Performance Accountability Questions:

8

1. Who are our customers?

2. How can we measure if our customers are better off? (*Is anyone better off? measures*)

3. How can we measure if we are delivering services well? (*How well did we do it?* measures)

4. How are we doing on the most important of these measures? Baselines and Causes

5. Who are the partners that have a role to play in doing better?

6. What works to do better, including no cost and low-cost ideas? (Possible actions)

7. What do we propose to do? (Action Plan)

Book Roadmap

This book chronicles my journey using RBA and the lessons I have learned through the development of Connecticut's CT Kids Report Card, and in creating the roadmap for implementation of RBA at DCF.

I have seen what RBA can do to transform a statewide agency for the better. Becoming an RBA practitioner has helped me to think and approach my work differently and more effectively by assessing whether our practices and programs lead to children and families being better off. You can make a difference by focusing on the right things.

So let's get started. Where do you want to lead your agency?

REFLECTIONS AND RECOMMENDATIONS

1. Do you remember why are you doing this work?

   Identify the main reason.

2. Does your work occur at the population level, the performance level or both?

   This is very important to understand. Identify where your work occurs.

3. What is the result you hope to achieve?

   Identify that result, using positive language, and keep it brief.

4. Who are the partners you will need to be successful?

   Identify them. As your work develops, you may decide you need more, or different, people at the table - that's ok.

5. How will you know you have achieved your result?

   Describe what success would look like.

Chapter 2

A Starting Place: How We Made the Connecticut Kids Report Card Happen

The People, the Plan, the Process

In Connecticut, as in most states, we spend a lot of money on services and programs for children and families. The total state resources allocated to promoting the well-being of children and families in fiscal year 2009 was nearly $5.62 billion.[2]

And we shouldn't be surprised at the number. Budgets reflect our priorities, and as a society we care a lot about our kids and the environment in which they grow up.

But what is confounding is that we didn't know whether we were getting our money's worth! Historically, we have been

---

2 Connecticut General Assembly. Final Report: RBA Pilot Project Study of Selected Human Services Programs (P.A. 09-166). Web. 15 January 2010 available at: http://www.cga.ct.gov/2009/pridata/Studies/PDF/RBA_Pilot_Study_FINAL_Committee_%20Report.PDF

hard pressed to determine whether all the spending and programs have made a difference for children and families, and whether anyone was better off as a result of the services delivered.

Without reliable and relevant metrics, we couldn't evaluate the progress of state policies. We couldn't tell our stakeholders - taxpayers, policymakers, voters, parents - how well we were doing. And in recent years, with state and local budgets shrinking and competition for limited funds growing, this was a big problem for any organization funded by the public, let alone a statewide network of service providers and agencies.

So we set out to develop a scorecard with considerable breadth to grade ourselves on all the state-funded services for children and families. We started at the population level, with the intent of drilling down into program performance as we began to learn more at the population level.

The CT Kids Report Card was developed in response to Connecticut *Public Act no. 11-109: An Act Requiring an Annual Results-Based Accountability Report Card Evaluating State Policies and Programs Impacting Children.*[3]

The public act was authored by Representative Diana Urban. Diana is a veteran legislator and a passionate advocate for children. In addition to serving as Co-Chair of the Children's Committee of the Connecticut General Assembly, she led the development of the CT Kids Report Card.

Our plan was to build a data-based guide for policy and program decisions to improve the quality of life of all Connecti-

---

3 See Appendix B.

cut children and to serve as an accessible, central source of information available on Connecticut children's well-being. The report card would help us look at program performance to determine whether our state was actually investing in programs that resulted in all Connecticut children growing up in stable living environments, safe, healthy and ready to lead successful lives.

What is now known as the CT Kids Report Card has begun to help us understand where things are working well, where things are not working well, where the gaps exist, and what we need to do to Turn the Curve for all children in Connecticut. It moves us toward stronger public accountability and serves as an effective tool for getting from talk to action.

Our Results Statement:

All Connecticut children grow up in stable environments, safe, healthy and ready to lead successful lives.

Table 1 - CT Kids Report Card Results Statement

As you can see, this results statement has four areas of focus: (1) stable, (2) safe, (3) healthy and (4) future success. In fact, we treat each of these areas as its own results statement, with headline and secondary indicators.

The real value of the CT Kids Report Card is that it is a collaborative effort. It has been developed in consultation with a working group of representatives of state agencies, the judiciary, community organizations, private service providers and program operators, parents and other caretakers of children, child advocacy organizations, health care and child-care professionals, K-12 schools, and universities. Additionally, having a legislatively-led process that includes all three branches of government helped bring everyone to the table.

With that being said, early in the process I joined a small group of public and private professionals who emerged as team leaders in the work, including Brian Hill from the state Judicial Branch; Erica Bromley, an independent consultant; and Christine Dauser, director of a mental health clinic for children. I served as the fourth team leader. The group was committed to the goals of the CT Kids Report Card legislation, and also understood the basics of RBA. We each led our own team on one of the four focus areas referenced within the results statement: safety, stability, health and future success.

These teams were made up of volunteers from a larger working group. Each team was comprised of regular people who came together to develop headline and secondary indicators, locate data, and establish their data development agenda.

Our group coordinated these data sources and communicated issues on a regular basis. We learned about and agreed to report data in the accepted format for each discipline. And we shared a commitment to discerning what the data could tell us as well as what it couldn't.

Original duties of the group included: (1) ensuring the data were relevant, accurate, and understandable now and in the future; (2) committing to update the data annually; and (3) converting technical language to plain language without compromising accuracy. The group put in a tremendous amount of work for the first two years of report card development and laid the foundation for progress that continues today.

In addition to the team leaders, two more members of the group served as our coach and our coordinator. Jill Jensen served in the Office of Program Review and Investigation at Connecticut's General Assembly for over thirty years before retiring shortly after the RBA report card law was passed. After retiring, Jill stayed involved as a coordinator to keep us all on track. Bennett Pudlin from the Charter Oak Group served as our RBA coach and gave us support and guidance in applying RBA to the work. Jill and Bennett's support was indispensable. This group, led by Representative Urban, all worked together to help advance the CT Kids Report Card.

This self-selecting group serves as a testament to how RBA makes it possible to jump into the work in a meaningful way pretty quickly. And once in the work it requires honesty, commitment and teamwork.

Is it simple? Yes.
Is it important? Yes.
Is it easy? No.

If it's not easy, why use RBA to develop the report card?

Because it enables us to address whole populations as well as program performance at the same time. We can target spending to programs that work to help us Turn the Curve in underperforming systems. This means we have greater accountability when it comes to getting better results for our children. And this is especially true given that the current economy with tighter budgets is the new normal. Investing taxpayer dollars in efforts that improve outcomes for children and families is more important than ever.

We knew the stakes were high. Because the CT Kids Report Card was one of the earlier statewide RBA projects in Connecticut, some partners didn't know what to expect. In fact, many of the service providers working directly with children and families were nervous about whether the RBA process would lead to a decrease in their own funding or services. We realized that we had to establish some ground rules and operating assumptions as we began this work. They included the following:[4]

The Ground Rules

1. No one program or agency can be held solely responsible for large systems change.

2. Funders and providers are partners in this work, working to achieve the same outcomes for the clients they serve.

3. The lack of desired performance outcomes does not necessarily mean a program, a provider, or a service type has failed. Rather, performance data should be used to inform next steps and not to punish providers for "poor performance."

---

4 These ground rules were further developed in a guide for implementing RBA by a small team made up of representatives of public and private agencies – including all three branches of government, advocacy groups, and consultants. The further developed work can be found in Appendix F at the end of this book.

These ground rules were incredibly valuable in creating an open and collaborative environment. The RBA process can't work if partners are afraid of being singled out or not comfortable sharing their honest assessments. The ground rules you adopt may be different, but I recommend making these principles clear and accepted as you build your network of partners and stakeholders.

In addition to setting ground rules, another consideration for this work is avoiding burnout. Not surprisingly, all the members of our working group were busy professionals in their own right. Although their enthusiasm never waned, after a couple of years the extra work began to take its toll. The recommendation for other groups starting a similar process is to give some thought to setting set-term limits.

Outside Support

During the process of building the CT Kids Report Card, we received a tremendous amount of support from two training and consulting groups: Clear Impact, formerly Results Leadership Group, and the Charter Oak Group. In addition to their skills, they are extremely generous with their time and their expertise. I can't speak highly enough about these groups and the support and guidance that each of them provided.

The Charter Oak Group has provided training and guidance about RBA, the results, indicators, and data, and coordination with other entities engaged in similar work. Their assistance really made a difference in moving our work forward. They have helped me, and many other new RBA practitioners understand RBA, identify population indicators and program performance measures, and grapple with some of the more challenging aspects of implementation. They also provided ongoing technical assistance, and in general, served as professional and gentle coaches when we needed it.

Clear Impact provided us with Clear Impact Scorecard™ ("Scorecard") software to manage our large data set and with technical assistance to help us with the display and tracking of our data. They provided options for structuring multiple results and indicators on the Scorecard and helped the Connecticut General Assembly IT staff post data on its public website.

We used the Scorecard to develop the CT Kids Report Card and to organize and report indicators on an ongoing basis. We found that, like RBA, the focus of the Scorecard is effectiveness. It allows us to organize and share indicator data easily.

As we proceed, the Scorecard will give us the ability to track progress, look at data on multiple levels, and jointly manage how we are doing to Turn the Curve for Connecticut's children.

REFLECTIONS and RECOMMENDATIONS

1. Is there a population level result to which your agency's work contributes?

   If not, consider working with partners to develop one.

2. Who is missing from your population level planning table?

   When the table is truly full, decisions may take longer, but your strategies will have more traction because more people will have had the opportunity to be part of the process. Including more people in population level planning also increases the likelihood that you will address areas of conflict earlier. You may be surprised by who shows up at first, who keeps showing up, and where you find your allies.

3. Have you appointed a coordinator for your project?

If this is a statewide (or equivalent) level project, don't underestimate the amount of work that coordination involves. Your coordinator does not necessarily need to be the actual leader of the project, but he or she should be someone who can keep everyone on track, coordinate across agencies, and understand the data reporting conventions.

4. Is your report card turning into a "gotcha,"?

Reread the ground rules outlined earlier in this chapter. State agencies and their providers will need to share the good, the bad, and the ugly if the report card is going to be effective. Remember, lack of desired outcomes does not automatically mean a provider or a service didn't work. These are important services and there are always positives and ways to get better. (As Mark Friedman reminds us, if a fire department isn't performing well, you don't get rid of the department. You fix it.)

5. Are your partners burning out?

Consider setting term limits. Let new partners take on tasks after a set amount of time (a couple of years at most). Not only will you preserve your team, but you will solidify your progress, and you will allow additional partners to share their talents and develop their RBA skills.

6. Have you asked for help?

There is a growing field of consultants with RBA expertise who can help you develop your work. The insight and experience of someone who has wrestled with the same challenges can be valuable in moving past roadblocks.

7. Have you considered tools like the Scorecard software to manage and track data, as well as create transparent action plans that can be shared publicly?

Having a common tool, that can be accessed by all partners and shared with the public, can make shared management and communication easier and much more effective.

Chapter 3

Moving Forward:
Using RBA to Align the Report Card and Departmental Work

The Department of Children and Families -
An Overview

The Department of Children and Families ("DCF") has five mandated areas: responsibility for Connecticut's child protective services, children's behavioral health, education for children in its care, prevention, and responsibility for Connecticut's committed delinquents. The Department operates three facilities, including the Albert J. Solnit Children's Psychiatric Center (North Campus in East Windsor and the South Campus in Middletown), the Connecticut Juvenile Training School in Middletown, and the Wilderness School in East Hartland.

The Department also consists of a Central Office and fourteen Area Offices that are organized into six regions. With a staff of over 3,200, approximately 100 types of contracted services, and numerous private agencies as provider partners, DCF is responsible for providing supervision and services to 36,000 children and 16,000 families across its programs and mandate areas each year.

Operating an agency of this size and scope is no small challenge. And the ability to measure and manage performance is central to public accountability. So the prospect of RBA coming to DCF was an important development for the agency. Here are the four factors that drove the timing of RBA at DCF.

Four changes that brought RBA to DCF

In 2011, The Honorable Joette Katz stepped down from the Connecticut Supreme Court to become Commissioner of DCF. Commissioner Katz quickly established herself as a leader and an agent of change regarding the focus and performance of the department. One of those changes included the Commissioner's public commitment to making DCF an RBA agency.[5]

When Commissioner Katz arrived at DCF she quickly engaged many stakeholders, from inside and outside the agency, in examining current practice and performance. She encouraged an expanded focus on more than just compliance with federal oversight, which had previously consumed much of the agency's work.

---

5 Recently, the Annie E. Casey Foundation released a report about the change at the Department of Children and Families led by Commissioner Katz. The Connecticut Turnaround - The Annie E. Casey Foundation (The Annie E. Casey Foundation) *available at*: http://www.aecf.org/resources/the-connecticut-turnaround/

Commissioner Katz invited us to start thinking about children thriving and being prepared for adulthood, and working with families as partners in developing solutions instead of seeing families as the problem. In effect, we began to think about what it really means for children and families to be better off after involvement with DCF.

Second, *Public Act 11-109: An Act Requiring an Annual Results-Based Accountability Report Card Evaluating Policies and Programs Impacting Children*[6] strengthened the use of RBA in Connecticut. The CT Kids Report Card gained traction, in part, because of the consistent message that, "RBA isn't a gotcha." No one should use RBA on a witch-hunt to cut funding or to cast blame.

Third, the Connecticut General Assembly's Legislative Program Review and Investigations Committee and the analysts in its Office of Program Review and Investigations ("PRI") began to use an RBA approach in their studies of DCF. This was an incredibly powerful validator, given that the purpose of PRI is to "determine whether state programs and policies are effective, continue to serve their intended purposes, are carried out efficiently and effectively, or require modification or elimination."[7] A few of these staff members were particularly helpful in engaging state agency partners in identifying performance measures that improve outcomes for children.

Last, but definitely not least, the Appropriations Committee of the Connecticut General Assembly began requiring RBA report cards on specific programs from a number of state

---

6 See Appendix B.
7 PRI - Connecticut General Assembly (PRI - Connecticut General Assembly) http://www.cga.ct.gov/pri/mission.asp

agencies. The Appropriations Committee developed an RBA report card template for all agencies to use.[8]

With those four pillars in place, we laid the foundation for bringing RBA to DCF. But we knew that it was just the beginning.

REFLECTIONS and RECOMMENDATIONS

1. Do you have advocates for RBA at your agency?

   For agency-wide implementation you need the support and leadership of agency administration.

2. Do you have advocates for RBA outside of your agency?

   Having allies in the legislature and other agencies will help build support for the work and will also provide you with your own support system when you start using RBA.

---

8 See Appendix C

Chapter Four

Implementing RBA
Across the Department

Beginning the Work

Using the RBA approach, we started with the end in mind. Then we determined where we wanted to be, what that would look like, what our baseline performance was, and what we needed to do to Turn the Curve on our performance.

The implementation spanned the following areas:

1. Development of a DCF strategic plan and the use of RBA in the management of agency performance;

2. Staff, provider and community training and support;

3. The use of RBA to manage contracted services;

4. Getting from Talk to Action.

I'll cover the first two areas in this chapter and the last two in Chapter 5.

Development of DCF Strategic Plan and the Management of Agency Performance

The DCF strategic plan was developed in alignment with the following population results statement from the CT Kids Report Card:

Results Statement:
Connecticut children grow up in stable environments, safe, healthy, and ready to lead successful lives.

DCF developed its contribution to the results statement referencing all four of its focus areas:

DCF's Contribution to the Results Statement:
Working together with families and communities for children who are healthy, safe, smart and strong.

DCF's identified partners included families, community agencies, faith-based agencies, schools, and advocates. Working with those partners, the Department identified seven cross-cutting priorities for approaching the work:

1. Implementing strength-based family policy, practice and programs;

2. Applying the neuroscience of early childhood and adolescent development;

3. Expanding trauma-informed practice and culture;

4. Addressing racial inequities in all areas of our practice;

5. Building new community and agency partnerships;

6. Improving leadership, management, supervision and accountability; and

7. Becoming a learning organization.

These priorities were woven into nine strategies designed to improve DCF's performance and contribute to the population level result:

1. Increase investment in prevention and health promotion;

2. Apply strength-based, family-entered policy, practice and supports agency-wide;

3. Develop or expand regional networks of in-home and community services;

4. Congregate rightsizing and redesign;

5. Address the needs of specific populations;

6. Support collaborative partnerships with communities and other state agencies;

7. Support public and private sector workforce development;

8. Increase the management capacity of DCF to manage both ongoing operations *and* change; and

9. Improve revenue maximization and develop reinvestment priorities and methods.

The Commissioner prioritized these strategies by identifying annual performance expectations with agency-wide performance measures.

In addition to our internal RBA work, we developed RBA performance measures for our contracted services. The joint focus on the internal work and contracted services helped to ensure that both sets of work are related, and that the contracted services support the agency effort in contributing to the population result of all Connecticut children growing up in stable environments, being safe, healthy, and ready to live successful lives.

We benefited from early focus on our contracted services that gave our staff members a chance to participate in the development of performance measures that were distinct from their own day-to-day work.

By the time the Commissioner outlined that first set of RBA-formatted annual performance expectations (based on the strategic priorities), most of our managers had at least some experience applying RBA to our contracted services. They had already begun Turn the Curve thinking before they had to apply it to their own work.

Leaders from each region, operating division, and facility developed their own operational strategies with performance measures designed to help achieve the performance expectations. Management teams analyzed baseline data and worked to identify the story behind the baseline, as the first steps in developing their specific strategies and performance measures.

Some teams easily adapted to RBA and developed creative and integrated plans. They were able to find partners in other parts of the agency and beyond. The RBA approach, and in particular, the Turn the Curve exercise, was extremely useful in helping teams identify their primary customers, develop their "better off" measures, and design strategies to achieve those measures.

But other teams needed more support. Putting process-oriented thinking aside can be a real challenge for teams at large agencies. These teams benefit from having access to an RBA practitioner to help them switch to outcome-focused thinking in order to develop their "better off" measures.

As I mentioned earlier, RBA is simple, but it is not easy. This was no exception. But it is exciting and rewarding for a team when its players can analyze their data (really dig into it) and then identify potential strategies to Turn the Curve on their performance. And one experience stands out in illustrating why that excitement is justified.

A regional management team was working to increase the number of children living at home with their families. Its task required analyzing data about children in out-of-home care. The data were disaggregated by sex, race, and ethnicity.

The team noticed that one group of children - Latino boys - accounted for a significantly higher portion of the out-of-home population than all the rest. The team members dug into the data a little further and realized that these kids were *entering* care at the same rate as other children, but they were *remaining in* care for a longer time.

Further analysis of services available to the children and their families, after a return home, showed that these children were returning to homes needing bilingual services, which didn't exist. Without those services in the community, children remained in care for longer periods of time while services were sought.

Armed with this new discovery, the regional team developed a strategy that would have real impact. The team reached out to its providers and the larger community to collaborate on the creation of bilingual services.

Staff, Provider, and Community Training and Support

Quite frankly, when we started the RBA work at DCF, many people in our department had never heard of RBA. We had not been a data focused agency, so many of our managers were not comfortable analyzing data to manage agency performance. One manager even thought RBA was a new type of accounting procedure!

Additionally, until recently, DCF had long assigned management level staff members to oversee contracted services without providing standardized training in service management and oversight until recently. As you may have experienced in your agency, staff members assigned to manage services may not have the training or experience to oversee contracts, analyze data, or manage provider performance.

With the Commissioner's new approach and DCF's adoption of RBA, we knew that our management teams, program leads and provider partners needed to understand the RBA approach. So we made training a priority for both DCF staff and our provider partners. That way they could all understand a common language and jointly develop RBA performance measures. Together, they are now using performance data to manage and improve performance internally and for our contracted services.

But with only one person in the agency assigned to implement RBA, and a very tight budget, getting people trained required some creativity.

Luckily, Connecticut has two great RBA resources. One of those is the Charter Oak Group, which I mentioned in Chapter Two. The partners - Bennett Pudlin, Ron Schack, and Barry Goff - have been a tremendous asset to many public and private agencies seeking to understand and implement RBA.

The other resource, which is supported in large part by the Charter Oak Group, is the Connecticut RBA Practitioner Network. It is free to join and is an affiliation of people in Connecticut practicing RBA and interested in learning more about RBA. The network meets on a quarterly basis, and in different locations throughout the state to discuss topics of interest to the members. It also delivers free RBA 101 training on a regular basis.

The practitioner network has been helpful to my RBA work, and it is also a great training resource for DCF and provider partners. By offering to help coordinate meetings and register training participants, I had flexibility choosing locations that would be convenient for DCF staff and partners.

When possible, I try to schedule trainings at the DCF area offices or locations that our local staff use for training because we can use community connections that are already established with facility liaisons and building staff. This approach has made it easier to coordinate training for DCF staff and providers along with other agencies and nonprofit organizations.

The network relies on free training space, and will reserve ten seats in the class for the host agency if it provides an appropriate training location for fifty people. Not a bad deal.

As with learning most new things, the RBA101 class is a great introduction. But most people I know need some additional coaching and support as they begin RBA work. Developing ongoing internal support was an important next step.

Developing an Internal Support System for RBA

As soon as enough people were trained and beginning to use RBA, we developed an internal RBA affinity group at DCF. An affinity group is a group of colleagues who come together on a regular basis to explore common areas of practice within a specific body of work, with the goal of increasing knowledge and improving performance.

The DCF RBA affinity group meets quarterly to discuss topics of interest related to RBA, provide peer support to RBA practitioners within DCF, and offer training opportunities for DCF RBA practitioners. Training topics are designed around challenges that people have identified, themes that arise, and specific requests for training.

Before the first meeting of the RBA affinity group, we administered a survey to find out what kind of RBA-related topics participants were interested in learning more about; what they were struggling with; and in which areas they would like some topical training. In addition to understanding the needs of the group, the survey helped set the agenda for the first few meetings.

Instead of using the agency's RBA point person to lead the discussion, we engaged the group members themselves. At our first two meetings, we had RBA practitioners from within DCF present the work they had performed for the department so that their colleagues could actually see what RBA looked like in action.

That approach not only provided attendees with a chance to learn about a coworker's achievements with RBA, but it also generated a lot of questions around (and even challenges to) the presenter's RBA project. Although this was probably a little intimidating for some presenters, it gave others in the group an opportunity to help answer the questions and for participants to work through topics as a group. Those topics included the value of participant feedback and satisfaction, using a survey to gauge staff understanding about a particular service, and using informal data as the basis for a strategy to Turn the Curve on performance.

The members with advanced RBA training and experience guided the discussion and jumped in when it started veering off track. Overall it allowed coworkers to test out their understanding of RBA and help each other in the learning process.

REFLECTIONS and RECOMMENDATIONS

1. Are you creating an environment to inspire change?

Change is hard for all of us; in a bureaucracy it is really hard. Realize that for some of your colleagues it will take a while for them to make or accept change. In the meantime, begin working with co-workers who are excited about the change. It will take time, but others will follow after they see a new framework in action. Also consider creating an internal support group to endorse and support your agency-wide RBA work.

2. Are you building support for change when it does occur?

Change comes in baby steps. Build in more support and training than you think you will need:

- Reinforce how RBA provides a framework to connect individual projects to a larger whole. Consistently stress the focus on whether anyone is better off.

- Follow the introduction with training that uses specific and concrete examples for your type of work.

- Be prepared to provide a lot of technical assistance.[9]

If at all possible, assign a key staff member as your RBA point person to provide guidance, deliver training and technical assistance, and help keep the focus on "better off" measures.

---

9   I have included two presentations in Appendix D and E that demonstrate how the Department introduced, and then trained on, the development and use of performance measures.

Get connected with other professionals and agencies engaged in RBA work. If there is no existing network, consider forming a loosely affiliated group to provide support and informal training.

3. Are you creating opportunities for your staff to be trained on RBA?

Your staff will benefit from participating in RBA efforts that are indirectly related to their work before they start developing their own strategies and performance measures. The preparation will allow them to gain experience before they have to apply RBA to their own work.

Chapter Five

Managing Departmental Performance

Contracted Services

As an agency, DCF has invested significant time, talent and effort into developing RBA performance measures for our contracted services, of which DCF has approximately 100 different types. Those contracted service types include in-home evidence-based practices, outpatient behavioral health treatment, parent support programs, and many others.

Most service types have multiple contractors and locations. Often, these contractors provide direct services to the populations we're trying to reach. An initial review of the agency's contracts library showed that almost every service type had a "client outcome" section as part of the contract. As a term, "client outcome" is often used the same way as a "better off" measure is, so this should have been good news.

But on closer inspection, many of the items identified as outcomes did not measure whether anyone was better off or even provide any kind of "customer outcome" - core standards within the RBA framework. In fact, many of them were not performance measures at all.

It was clear we had some work to do.

Cataloging Outcomes

Ensuring that all contracts had RBA performance measures required cataloging and classifying the existing "performance measures."

That way we would know the extent of the task before us and could begin creating our approach to developing the right performance measures. We needed these measures to understand the impact of our contracted services in helping to ensure that Connecticut's children are healthy, safe, smart, and strong. We also had to understand what changes might be needed to deliver the best services possible to help achieve that end. That end could not be attained without using contractor performance data to manage performance.

This was every bit of the heavy lift it seemed to be. We had to scour every service contract for performance measures. We then cataloged all of the performance measures we found.

The cataloging process involved analyzing each performance measure to determine whether the measure could be considered a "how much," a "how well," or a "better off" measure. Not surprisingly, many of the existing "measures" didn't fit any of those categories. Rather, they either described components of the program or were what I started calling "contract compliance items." This latter category doesn't really measure performance (measures are always numbers, percentages, rates or ratios). Instead, it describes or clarifies a deliverable, such as hours of operation, program schedule, or the program design. And although contract compliance items are important, they are not performance measures and, therefore, belong in a different section of the contract.

All of the identified "outcomes" were catalogued, whether or not they were truly outcomes, contract compliance items, or descriptions of program components. That way we could get a sense of what we were tracking and holding contractors accountable for, or in other words, what we had been considering important.

As you can imagine, there was a lot of variety in what constituted "outcomes" in these contracts. In fact, the process identified twenty-two different categories of outcome or activity being measured, including one category for "no outcome identified."

In addition to giving us a good sense of our baseline, understanding the way people had categorized outcomes also informed where we would need to focus our training efforts. Now that we were beginning to understand the scope of the work ahead of us, the next step was to start setting priorities for performance measure development.

We prioritized the contracts by program or service type based on three criteria: (1) the program or service type's importance to the Commissioner's goals; (2) the amount of money spent on the program or service type; and (3) the number of locations where the program or service was being offered. Based on those criteria, we ranked programs as higher, medium, or lower priority.

In Connecticut, we fund a lot of evidence-based and promising practices. Because these programs generally have solid performance measures as part of their design, we ranked most of the evidence-based programs as lower priority for this task. We did this not because we felt they weren't important or that they necessarily had good "better off" measures, but because they had a strong foundation of performance measurement. In that sense, they were less urgent, and we felt more confident that we were already able to measure the performance of those programs better than many other programs.

After our initial three-tier prioritization of programs, we performed a second ordering of each program by the level of effort it would take to modify the outcome section so that it would be RBA-compatible.

While the majority of programs did not have RBA performance measures, some of them had measures that were close to a correct format. These would only need minor tweaking to create performance measures that included how much work was being done, how well it was being done, and whether anyone was better off as a result of program participation.

We rated programs a "1" if it would not take a lot of work to change their performance measures; a "2" if it needed a moderate amount of work but not an entire overhaul; and a "3" for programs that would need a significant amount of effort to develop appropriate performance measures. (see Table 1, pg. 40).

After determining the ranking by importance and by required effort for all of the programs, we began to combine the two rankings to determine the order in which we would proceed. We decided to start with the programs ranked highest priority and relative ease: those with a ranking of "H-1." That way we could create traction and impact while still addressing the work in a reasonable way and at a realistic rate.

Table 1 - Sample RBA Development Priority Matrix

Priority Level H = high, M = medium, L = low	Service Type	# of Programs	Program Lead	Dept Head	Annual Budget	RBA Prep Rating (work to be done) 1 = minimal, 2 = moderate, 3 = substantial
H	Community Based Life Skills	15	xxxxxxx	xxxxxxx	$980,868	3
H	Community Support for Families	8	xxxxxxx	xxxxxxx	$8,111,385	1
H	EMPS Crisis Intervention Service	6	xxxxxxx	xxxxxxx	$9,420,015	1
H	EMPS - Crisis Intervention Service System -Statewide Call Center	1	xxxxxxx	xxxxxxx	$616,446	1
H	Extended Day Treatment Program	16	xxxxxxx	xxxxxxx	$6,526,371	1
H	Family and Community Ties	6	xxxxxxx	xxxxxxx	$1,440,000	1
H	Juvenile Sexual Treatment	1	xxxxxxx	xxxxxxx	$314,456	2
H	Multi-dimensional Family Therapy (MDFT) Consultation and Evaluation	1	xxxxxxx	xxxxxxx	$1,004,183	1

The priority matrix gave us a starting point for the performance measure development work with our staff and provider partners. We pulled together DCF staff and providers to talk about RBA and discuss DCF's use of RBA in the context of population work (i.e., the CT Kids Report Card), agency-wide work (i.e., the DCF strategic plan and annual performance expectations), and then specifically how DCF was implementing RBA with our programs and contracted services.

The conversations with staff and providers also gave us the opportunity to reinforce two messages: first, that all of our efforts - including contracted services - are designed to contribute to the result that all of Connecticut's children live in stable environments, are safe, healthy, and ready to lead successful lives. Second, the conversations reminded us that the reason why we all got into this work was to change things for the better.

The alignment of all our efforts to that population result is a tangible, concrete way to make the change we all seek. People heard the message, and many of them understood the importance of this opportunity and began to work together to transform our system.

We wanted everybody to have a good understanding of the overall RBA effort across the department, the scope of the effort, and where they fit into the process. The importance of this last aim can't be overstated. Giving people a sense of where their work fits in with the larger process contributes to their sense of purpose and to the success of the effort.

A small team led the effort to develop performance measures. The team included two members of the agency's contracting division and me as the agency RBA point person. That inter-division partnership served to build traction across multiple divisions at the same time. This led to additional opportunities to introduce more people to the work, both inside and outside the agency. We were also able to identify additional programs and initiatives that could benefit from RBA-based thinking.

Members of that small team met with program leads and provider partners to introduce the concept of RBA performance measures. Later, that same team lead groups through the process of identifying "better off" measures, followed by the "how much" and "how well" measures.

These meetings reinforced the importance of starting with the end in mind. Often, our conversations started with "Tell me why we are funding this service" and "What does success look like for your clients?" Beginning the conversation this way kept people focused on what they wanted to achieve rather than what they did. There were even a couple of times when focusing on the "better off" measures led to some changes in program design.

These conversations were usually well received, and although some providers were concerned about potential "gotchas," making sure we focused on the right levels of accountability and responsibility helped to allay concerns.

We began to organize the programs and services into general service categories and catalog all of the RBA performance measures for services in each general category - similarly to how we cataloged the original "contract outcomes". The measures were cataloged using language that was general enough to be relevant for multiple program types. This has given us a good resource for the development of performance measures for new services, and it will also allow us to survey the breadth of our performance measures to ensure we really are measuring the right things and measuring them right.

An example of these performance measures is included on page 44:

Getting From Talk to Action

After launching into a campaign to establish an outcome-driven culture, train people on RBA, and develop RBA performance measures in all of our contracts, it would have been easy to fool ourselves into thinking we were done! But we were really just getting started.

Once you build an RBA culture, determine your desired results, establish the performance measures in your internal work and contracts, and train your staff and partners, you still have to move from talk to action.

There is often a big, collective sigh of relief when performance measures are completed. But we can't assume that the natural response of a bureaucracy will be to use those performance measures to understand and manage the performance of contracted agencies.

We knew that we couldn't just implement new practices. We had to build an ongoing support for, and management of, the new practices. For our regional, divisional, and facility management teams, quarterly performance reviews with the Commissioner and her team provide an opportunity to present performance data and to have meaningful conversations about what those data reflect, where performance needs to improve, and where the team's efforts are making a difference and turning a curve.

Figure 1. Performance Measures by Service Type

Service Type (Inlcudes multiple programs)	Programs included in Sevice Type	How much did we do? (Quantity of Work)	How well did we do it? (Quality of Work)	Is anyone better off? (Client Outcomes)	Data Sources Data sources does not necessarily mean every program's data source is identified here, but at least the data source for one program in this category is listed here
Behavioral Health Services	• Crisis Stabilization • EMPS - Crisis Intervention Service Systel Statewide Call Center • EMPS Crisis Intervention Service • Extended Day Treatment • Functional Family Therapy (FFT) • Intensive In-Home Child and Adolescent Psychiatric Services (IICAPS) • Juvenile Sexual Treatment (JOTLAB) New Haven • Muiltidimensional Treatment Foster Card • Outpatient Psychiatric Clinic for Children • Community Support Team • NH AO • Short-term Family Integrated Integrated Treatment (SPIT)	• Number of clients served annually • Number of family engagement activities • Number of family therapy sessions conducted • Number of aftercare activities conducted	• Percent of participants served who successfully complete treatment • Percent of families who complete treatment successfully and have a service length of stay between 120-160 days • Percent of participants served who are successfully linked to community bases services and/or pro-social supports • Percent of children/youth served for whom psychiatric hospitalization during the course of services is avoided • Percent of children/youth for whom an out-of-home placement during the course of services is avoided • Percent of families and caregivers completing the Ohio Scales at intake and at discharge • Percent of participants not arrested while receiving services • Percent of biopsychosocial assessments completed • Percent of family assessments completed • Percent of families engaged in treatment • Percent of youth maintaining continuity with their school program • Percent of youth discharged in 15 days or less • Percent of youth and families completing satisfaction surveys at discharge • Percent of youth and families engaged in aftercare activities	• Percent of participants who demonstrate increased functioning • Percent of participants who demonstrate decrease in problem severity • Percent of participants who met treatment goals • Percent of participants who remain in the community • Percent of participants in an academic or vocational program at the time of discharge • Percent of youth and their families who report improved communication and improved hope for the future • Percent of families evidencing improved family functioning • Percent of youth and families with enhanced social supports/community resources at discharge • Percent of positive family satisfaction • Percent of positive youth satisfaction • Percent of youth discharged to their placement of origin	PSDCRS

44

For contracted services, performance management includes an agency-level review of RBA report cards, acknowledgement of good performance, and understanding of poor performance. It also presents opportunities to recommend changes in practices, funding, program design, or when absolutely necessary, to change contractors. The internal management group described in the next section provides the home for ongoing performance review and management of our contracted services.

The Connecticut General Assembly has been requiring RBA report cards for some of our programs for the past four years. Until recently, this has caused a great deal of angst, including panicked pleas for assistance from program leads required to submit report cards.

After we provided consistent training for all of our program leads and began to require regular RBA report cards that included actions to Turn the Curve, we saw consistent improvement in our program leads' ability to analyze program performance. I get fewer requests for help in developing RBA report cards these days, and that's a good thing.

This new wave of understanding and managing performance is leading to real, practical actions to improve performance. In 2015, we implemented the requirement for all program leads to develop and submit quarterly RBA report cards for all the services they oversee. Again, this was pretty stressful the first time, but as they began to pay attention to the data, the program leads started identifying lots of performance issues - some good, and others that require new and different efforts to improve performance.

Some types of performance issues our program leads have identified through their analysis of performance data include the following:

- Access to evidence-based services based on race and ethnicity

- The rate of successful program completion

- The percent of foster care providers receiving training

- The effectiveness of targeted services to keep young children with significant behavior problems in school

Sometimes the report cards that I consider the best show performance trends that are much less than ideal; things like low rates of successful completion, or low utilization. What makes those report cards so good is that they show us where we need to focus our efforts to Turn the Curve. Identification of performance issues and trends gives program leads and provider partners clear direction on where to focus their efforts to understand the story behind the baseline and to identify actions to Turn the Curve, based on that story.

Creating a Culture of Performance Management

DCF has an internal management group that meets regularly to review its contracted services and the effectiveness of those services. For the last four years this effort has included building a department-wide internal structure and culture through which we have begun to regularly review program performance, client outcomes, and program funding. A group like this can drive performance management in at least four ways:

1. It provides a sense of legitimacy and helps staff members understand that this is a department-wide effort and has the support of agency leadership.

2. It helps to establish and develop buy-in from other agency managers who may not really understand RBA, or who may not be fully invested in performance measure development and performance management.

3. It serves as a place to identify drawbacks with potential performance measures, data sources, and reporting formats.

4. Most importantly, it provides an agency-level review and assessment of program performance that identifies those programs that are working. And by also identifying programs that need improvement, it can serve as a forum to manage the overall service system.

Any way you slice it, it's a good idea to use a group like this to introduce and endorse your efforts. It can experiment with ideas and help you anticipate where your implementation battles will likely be. Just remember to keep the group focused on performance and performance measures, and on providing feedback that will help with the management of contracted services.

Using Data to Manage Performance

As I noted earlier, the evidence-based services DCF funds did not necessarily have RBA performance measures. But they did measure both the quantity and quality of services delivered. They also regularly reviewed performance. Program leads, providers, and representatives of the services were already meeting to analyze data to improve performance.

Developing RBA report cards for these evidence-based services was easier than starting from scratch with other programs because they already measured performance. Additionally, their collaborative approach to data review was a good model for other program leads who were starting to use performance data.

For many other program types, and program leads, beginning to measure and manage performance was a new approach to the work, and for many colleagues it was pretty intimidating. In fact, about a year ago, I approached a colleague about an RBA report card he had worked on, and that had some pretty big inconsistencies. As I tried to engage him in a conversation about the data, he held up his hand, and informed me "Anne - I don't DO data. That's why I became a social worker." Then he smiled and walked away.

As shocking as I found that approach, I encountered similar situations on other occasions. Program leads would come to a data meeting to present a program's performance, and would come *without* data, just planning to have a conversation.

As DCF began to change the conversation around performance, the approach, and expectations and support for our own staff, we began to see changes in how more program leads began to think and talk about services.

I finally realized that people were beginning to understand the value of performance data when I walked past a meeting room and heard part of a conversation that included the following: "We have the data, but maybe we are measuring the wrong things. If we are trying to ensure that kids are better off after our services, we need to be measuring different things."

Success!

Similarly, our regional, divisional, and facility management teams are focusing on their strategies to improve internal performance. As part of that effort, each management team meets with the Commissioner and her team on a quarterly basis. At that meeting they present their performance data showing how much they are doing, how well they are doing it, and whether anyone is better off. They identify and report on strategy modifications when their original strategies didn't create the desired change. As our staff have become more comfortable with understanding data, they have begun to see how analyzing their performance helps them to identify what they are doing right and what they need to improve. They have also begun to create better ways to collect and understand data so that they can better understand the story behind the baseline and address underlying issues that affect performance.

Accountability and Responsibility

Let me pause here and refer to a proposition I made at the beginning of this book: that we all get into this work because we want to change the world. That premise applies to both state agency staff and provider staff. Part of changing the world is understanding how your small contribution is part of a larger contribution. That concept is clearly outlined in the RBA model, when you look at the relationship between performance accountability and population accountability.

Understanding that relationship makes it easier to appreciate appropriate attribution and responsibility. If you explain to someone where their contribution fits within the larger whole, they can see that there are also limits to performance accountability. Funders should not ask providers to be responsible for something over which they have no control or which is not part of their contractual agreement.

Talking about accountability - especially increasing the accountability of providers and agency staff - can cause tension. Providers may be concerned that the funder is going to use the new information developed through RBA implementation to punish them. And it can also be difficult for agency staff who may not have had to really look at data and work with providers to increase accountability.

All in all, for our system, this was something new. And in the past, the funder-provider relationship had not always worked as fairly or effectively as what we were proposing with RBA. Providers were aware of that.

To demonstrate the value of the RBA approach, I often tell this story:

I was sitting with a group of colleagues and we were talking about one particular service and discussing performance measures for that service. Some of the group expressed their dissatisfaction with the clients that the providers were serving. They were not happy with the selection process by which children were being accepted into the program. They felt providers were accepting the wrong children and not the children for whom the program had been designed. So we drilled that down a little bit more, and I asked them where the providers get the referrals.

It turned out that they got the referrals from us! Did they have the opportunity to turn down the client? No. In effect, we were holding our providers responsible for something they couldn't control, but that we could!

This situation is a good example of why it is important to get that relationship right in order to be good partners, to understand performance, and to measure the right things. You can imagine how telling this story reduces the anxiety in the room when we begin to look at performance measures and accountability together with our provider partners.

Understanding that accountability and responsibility go hand-in-hand makes it easier for us to start asking ourselves important questions: What is our (the funder's) end? Why are we funding the service? What are the outcomes we want for our clients? And what does that look like?

Next steps and continued learning

Now you're all caught up with our story. The RBA work at DCF continues today, so this is by no means the end of the story. In fact, our internal performance work and our contracted performance work continue to evolve. Likewise, there is continued development of the CT Kids Report Card. We continue to get better at using data to manage performance and learning from other public and private agencies. We have to ask ourselves tough questions, challenge assumptions, and shift away from doing things the way they've always been done; and we need to remember that change does not happen overnight! In fact, it is important to remember that change is a long term investment.

Implementing RBA in an agency is not a one-shot deal. It is a journey to a more effective way of doing the work. Using Turn the Curve thinking is helping us to measure the progress we are making each step of the way. Small changes each month don't always seem like much, but they add up over time, and when we look back after months of implementation, and we see data actually trending in the right direction, we realize how far we have come.

As a result of all our work, here are some measurable changes we've achieved in our own performance:

Management of Agency Performance

- 100% of program leads have been trained in RBA

- 90% of management staff members have been trained in RBA

- 100% of regional management teams, facility management teams, and centralized operations teams have developed operational strategies, with RBA performance measures

- 88% of teams are actively using RBA to manage performance

Contracted Services

- 90% of our contracted services have RBA performance measures; and 10% are being re-designed or re-procured, with RBA performance measures included in the new design;

- 100% of the Department's 33 program leads now use performance data to report on program performance;

- 70% of submitted RBA report cards have identified meaningful ways to Turn the Curve;

- 30% of the report cards identify significant data development agenda items;

As you can see, we have come a long way, and there are still many miles left on our journey.

REFLECTIONS and RECOMMENDATIONS

1. Do your service contracts include RBA performance measures?

   Systematically review your contracts, which includes cataloging and classifying existing performance measures, in order to establish your baseline. Then prioritize your work and systematically add the appropriate performance measures to each contract.

2. Are you working with provider partners and program leads to improve performance measures?

   Developing a performance measure catalog by general program type, or logical groupings of programs, can provide a useful reference and resource tool as you expand the work across your network of programs.

3. Are you using data to understand performance?

   Create an expectation for, as well as a practice of, sharing data. Use performance data to celebrate good performance and identify those areas in need of improvement.

Chapter 6

Nine Lessons Learned Along the Way

Training so many partners, providers and stakeholders in RBA has given me reason to reflect on my own progress with RBA. I recognize how long it took me to feel proficient. And looking back over the arc of my career, there are nine core lessons I'd like to share:

1. Change is Hard

Change is always hard when it's someone else's idea.

Early in my career, I had the opportunity to work as part of an interagency team on a community-based systems-change effort. The leader of the team identified us all as "change agents."

Then she warned us that people don't like change agents.

At the time, that didn't make a lot of sense to me because I knew we were going to help improve a number of systems in an effort that was designed to ultimately improve the quality of life across a community. How could people not want to embrace change?

That was before I had someone else's idea of positive change imposed on me and my work. Once change was imposed on me, I began to understand change a little differently.

When people have been doing something for a long time, they get good at it. And when they get good at it in a large agency, they get positive reinforcement. And when they get positive reinforcement, they have every reason to believe they are doing the right thing.

But when we introduce system change, we throw a curveball at those people, often without warning. Suddenly the message shifts from reinforcing what they have been doing to telling them they need to change what they are doing, the way they think about their work, and the way they measure success. That is hard for any of us!

Change is a wonderful thing - when it is your idea - and it can be very difficult when it's imposed on you. Not surprisingly, people resist unanticipated and uninvited change. That kind of resistance is an invisible, but important, institutional barrier, which you can ignore at your own peril.

Engage colleagues in the change effort by helping them to remember their reasons for getting into the work and the difference they wanted to make in the world. Then introduce RBA as an approach that focuses on whether their clients are better off as a result of their efforts.

Mark Friedman likes to show people how what they are already doing is valued and can be incorporated into the new way of doing the work. He tells people, "We don't throw anything away. Everything you are already doing fits somewhere in RBA."

Showing people that they and their work are valued, and helping them to reframe their thinking to focus on whether anyone is better off as a result of their efforts, can be useful in helping them understand and accept change.

2. Change Takes Support

You can't do it all without help.

It is a good idea to have someone in your agency as your RBA point person, who can guide the work and serve as the go-to person when people have RBA questions. Until everyone starts to understand how to use data to manage performance, it is too easy for the larger group to view RBA as a burden rather than a resource.

Until your colleagues feel comfortable with the work and their abilities, they will need regular assistance with the step-by-step implementation of strategies, the development of performance measures and report cards, and the usage of data to inform next steps.

3. Change Takes Time

Changing culture and performance in a large agency is like turning the *Queen Mary*.

It's also important to remember that change takes time. When we began to implement RBA at DCF, I would have said that, although there were plenty of early adopters, as a group, state agency managers were hard partners to engage. They were tougher than providers, community members, and direct service staff members. Some seemed set in their ways and were committed to doing business as usual, and a few of them had a difficult time understanding key RBA principles. However, once engaged, they began to focus on the outcomes they wanted to achieve and to develop effective strategies.

I use the analogy of turning around the 1,000 foot transatlantic ocean liner. It's a massive operation that takes a lot of time and patience. Over the last two years, I have come to understand that investments into state agency staff take a while to produce benefits. I've seen incredible growth in the appreciation for, and use of, a results-based management approach, but it took time to get to this point.

We began by introducing RBA as a new framework in 2011, and then provided training on how to use the RBA approach. That was followed up with ongoing technical assistance, peer support, and implementation. All in all, we spent approximately four years building agency capacity through training, technical assistance, contract amendments, and implementation in key areas throughout the agency. It wasn't until year five of the work that all of the efforts toward implementation became visible as a connected and coordinated agency-wide approach. These investments have all paid off in strengthening the understanding and application of RBA across this agency.

The change you seek happens incrementally - in baby steps. Be patient. These changes add up eventually.

4. Change Takes Training

Empower your staff and community partners by making sure they have the information they need to succeed

I can't stress enough the importance of providing training to your staff and to your provider partners. People have been hearing about RBA for years. And like a game of telephone, they don't always hear the message the way it was intended. Further, there are some important concepts and terms that are used in RBA, and it is very helpful to make sure everyone is speaking the same language and has the same understanding of concepts.

The good news is that there are plenty of training resources available, starting with Mark Friedman's book: *Trying Hard Is Not Good Enough*, and the RBA101 curriculum. But don't stop with those. I have found that new RBA practitioners - both in my agency and in the non-profit community - want training and support in developing performance measures and reporting their data.

Find out where people are struggling, and then seek out or develop training to meet their needs. At DCF, we began by first teaching staff and provider partners how to develop performance measures. That was followed by training on understanding, interpreting, and reporting performance data. The next round of training and support centered on using performance data to manage performance, and to identify actions to Turn the Curve.

As colleagues and partners become more proficient at the work, their training needs will change. Your training and support efforts will need to change with them.

5. Engage Group Effort and Find Partners

Results and performance are a group effort - no one person, program or agency is responsible for success or failure.

My boss, Deputy Commissioner Michael Williams, has an African proverb as part of his email signature: "If you want to walk fast, walk alone. If you want to walk far, walk with others." The scope and depth of the social impact we seek is more than we can take on as individuals. That is the inherent value of a community. We have the best chances of attaining our goals at the performance level and the population level when we prioritize our shared goals.

So share the burden and the credit. There is no "I" in team, right? Well, there is no "I" in RBA either. RBA work isn't about one person's work, vision, or priorities. RBA work is all about shared vision, shared accountability, and shared results.

Building the CT Kids Report Card was a cross-agency, multi-stakeholder process drawn together by many participants. The legislature, non-profit organizations, foundations, child-welfare advocates, and state agency staff all played a role. Why? Because they all wanted to improve outcomes for children and families in Connecticut.

Your partners are out there! Find them in other state agencies, nonprofits, and even other states. You can support each other, try out new ideas, and sometimes share the struggles of implementing a new way of doing business. Just talking with more people about implementing RBA creates a sense of momentum that is engaging. It helps contribute to the idea that we are part of a growing wave of new and effective ways of doing business.

When we began our strategic planning at DCF with an RBA approach, some of our agency staff had trouble wrapping their heads around the concept of starting with the end in mind versus "the work we do." They didn't necessarily see the immediate relevance of RBA to the work they did. But, most importantly, there was a smaller group of people who "got it" right away and became the core support for the initial work. Not only were they willing to invest the time in learning RBA, but they were also willing to start using it in their work.

When given the opportunity, build on the strengths of those early adopters and create a group of practitioners who can help to introduce and reinforce the work. With additional reinforcement, training, and support, the others will eventually follow.

6. View Your Work with a Wide-Angle Lens

Help people understand where they fit in the big picture and how RBA can work for them.

Initiatives like the CT Kids Report Card that aim for population level results involve partners across different agencies and service systems. Appreciating the full scope and combined impact of these projects, at the population level, requires a very wide lens and an understanding that the issues are much broader than what one agency can address. But the actual implementation of services that contribute to the population result is often performed by individual agencies. Consequently, we mixed the two together, and it took longer for us to get on track than it would have if we had a better understanding of alignment.

That relationship between population and performance work can feel like a disconnect and can breed misunderstanding. The problem occurs when people working within a system or agency think that RBA requires them to target their work to an entire population.

People don't always see how their work - oftentimes at the direct service level - is connected to a larger effort. They understand that their service leads to a relatively small number of participants being better off. However, when they have the opportunity to understand that their service is funded as part of a larger strategy, and that it is combined with other services that also create "better off" conditions for other participants, they can more easily appreciate the bigger effect.

When they see that there are multiple strategies, each with multiple efforts to create "better off" conditions for many more people, they begin to understand the power of RBA, the importance of performance level work, and how that performance level work is related to population level work.

When I was introduced to RBA, it was as part of an interagency strategic planning process, and we were all new to RBA. We didn't understand the difference between population level and performance level work. Even if we had, I am not sure we would have understood where our work fit. Consequently, we mixed the two together, and took longer to get on track than we would have with a better understanding of alignment.

During that strategic planning process, we changed steering committee members and introduced a new co-chair part of the way through. At her first meeting, while we were orienting the members to our RBA approach, the new co-chair jumped up and exclaimed, "We can't be responsible for all the kids and families in the state! Our work only deals with a small part of that population! There is no way our work will address all the needs!"

Of course, she was right, but she was never expected to shoulder all the responsibility! That was the day that I learned the importance of helping people understand where their work fits, and that no one person, agency, or group, is expected to carry the load alone.

7. Change Perspective

Change thinking from "what we do" to "what we want to achieve."

One of the biggest challenges for individuals working in government and non-profit agencies is to change the way they think about their work from "what we do" to "what we are trying to achieve."

In an advanced RBA training, Mark Friedman once explained how a simple questioning technique could help us change perspective on our fundamental assumptions. The technique, learned from Mark's friend and colleague Jolie Bain Pillsbury, involves asking "why?" five times to find the real answer you seek.

Originally conceived by the founder of Toyota Industries to find the root causes of manufacturing problems, the "5-Whys" analysis has now been widely adopted by management consultants in nearly every industry.

Mark uses the technique working on the story behind the baseline. And I've found it useful in helping people get to that elusive "better off" measure.

The following conversation is one that I had with an advocacy provider as she was beginning her RBA work:

Q1: "So, why are you doing parent outreach?"
A1: To get more parents involved in our groups.

Q2: "Why is that important?"
A2: So they can learn more about how the system works and what their rights are.

% who attended meetings who understand their rts

Q3: "Ok, why is it important for them to do that?"
A3: So they can become advocates for their children.

Q4: "Sounds good. Why is that important?"
A4: To make sure their kids get the services they are entitled to, and are able to participate in school and community activities. *(%)*

Q5: "Great! Anything else?"
A5: Being able to participate in school and community strengthens families. And strong families make strong communities - and strong communities make strong families. *(%) = better off*

You can see that a simple line of questioning was able to move us from a measure that was not a "better off" measure: # of parents who attended meetings, to four potential measures that are much stronger: 1) % of parents who attended meetings who understand their rights; 2) % of children who access the services they need; 3) school attendance; 4) % of children who participate in community activities on a regular basis.

8. Use Data to Tell Your Story

Data is a four-letter word...

Those of us in the human services field need to feel comfortable with, and be competent at, using data to assess needs, manage performance, and engage in effective planning.

Too often stakeholders are resistant (or perhaps afraid) of analyzing data. How many times have you heard people say something like my colleague did, "I don't do data - that is why I became a social worker."?

To be fair, working with data comes with its own challenges. You have to ensure the data are relevant, timely, accurate, and understandable. You have to establish clear standards for communicating, coordinating, and sharing data. Inconsistencies in datasets or the words we use to describe data can cause a lot of confusion. That's why RBA places such a premium on using easy-to-understand, accessible language and avoiding jargon when describing data. We have to understand what people mean when they use certain words. Otherwise, we are wasting our time.

The real promise of data is described by Commissioner Katz as being both a sword and a shield. Offensively, understanding quantitative and qualitative information empowers you to make to make strong, compelling arguments for improvements in programs. It is the currency that all of us working in the human services field trade in. And defensively, data can provide you with the authority and confidence to take unpopular positions. If the data show that a program isn't working, we can't afford to ignore that simply because the program has been around forever. Whether you're a policymaker, social scientist, program manager, service provider or advocate, you can appreciate the powerful role data can play in decision making.

9. Don't Wait to Start

As British author Samuel Johnson wrote back in the 1700s: "Nothing will ever be achieved if all possible objections must first be overcome."

You are going to make mistakes when you start the work. Don't let that stop you. As you grow in your understanding and appreciation of RBA, you will begin to realize your potential as an individual and to realize the potential of your organization. You'll notice that the size and scale of your mistakes shrink as your experience grows. You will also notice that you are beginning to Turn the Curve on some efforts. And for others, you will get better at identifying strategies to improve. That's a sign you're moving in the right direction.

Chapter 7

Final Reflection

Balancing the tension between urgent work and important work

Each of us working in the area of human services aims to evolve from "hard" work to "effective" work. Understanding the difference reveals the full power of RBA. But there is also another tension that threatens to derail our efforts: the difference between "urgent" work and "important" work.

Certainly, this distinction between the urgent and important is not a new concept. In 1954, President Eisenhower delivered a speech quoting the president of Northwestern University, noting this dilemma. He shared, "I have two kinds of problems, the urgent and the important. The urgent are not important, and the important are never urgent."

But managers in large agencies (even the White House) are drawn towards dealing with every day "emergency" issues.

And too often these "emergencies" could have been averted if those managers had been able to focus on what was important instead of what was urgent. The time wasted putting out fires, could be spent addressing the strategic and long-term important causes of these urgent issues. That poverty of time shortens our decision horizon.

So how do we stop what we must do in order to start what we should do? By building balance in our organizations. We delegate resources where they are appropriate. And for most of us, that means having someone in our agency tasked with looking at the important, strategic work exclusively - without risk of being pulled in to address the emergency of the day. This approach helps colleagues incorporate change-oriented approaches while not leaving urgent issues unattended.

The Beauty of Enlightened Ignorance

"True wisdom is knowing what you don't know" Confucius, *Sayings of Confucius*

We know that there is a great need for human services work. From child welfare to education to health and access to justice. Whether you live in Connecticut or California, the work we all do is driven by the need in our communities.

We also know that we don't always understand how to get the results that we want. We have the talent, effort and resources, but often we come up short in predictable ways. Either we struggle to understand the problem, or the solutions that we develop don't get us where we want to be.

If we're honest with ourselves, we can also admit there are probably things that we don't know that we don't know, and some that we are beginning to realize that we don't know. It's an acknowledgment that we don't have all the information or knowledge that we need. This is what we call "Enlightened Ignorance."

The concept of Enlightened Ignorance dates back to antiquity. It's the basis for the Socratic Method, the Greek philosopher's critical method of questioning that moves the questioner from a position of belief towards understanding truth, and it has very real implications for us to this day.

In order to answer the questions we want to answer in our daily work, and to make the changes we want to make, we really need to understand the information that is available to us. Sometimes we need to understand information that we are unable to access. Sometimes the information doesn't seem to make sense. Realizing that we don't know something important can make us feel powerless.

But we really aren't.

This is an important and intellectually powerful place to be. Your Enlightened Ignorance can help you formulate questions to help you better understand what you need to know. You can think of your enlightened ignorance the way we think of the data development agenda in RBA—what is it that you don't know and that you need to know?

Furthermore, using your Enlightened Ignorance will sometimes help you recognize that the problem you're trying to solve may not be the problem that your dataset has identified. Or that the solution that you've developed is not reflective of the real world challenge you're dealing with.

This is where the fun starts.

RBA helps us organize what we do know, and then take action in a disciplined way to fill in gaps in knowledge.

I encourage people to use their Enlightened Ignorance to guide their search for knowledge - or truth, as Socrates would say. Keep asking questions until they are answered - and answered in a way that you can understand. More often than not, this is easier than you think.

Remember that you don't need to be a subject matter expert or a data person to push for the answers you need; and when you are part of a team, you can utilize the strengths of other team members to retrieve and interpret confusing information.

Continuing Your RBA Journey

At the beginning of this book, I asked you to visualize the end result. What would happen if your agency Turned the Curve? How would the world, or at least your agency, be different if you were successful?

As Mark Friedman reminds us in *Trying Hard Is Not Good Enough*, results can change everything: "When people focus on the well-being of communities and customers, they reconnect to the reasons they became teachers, social workers, doctors, nurses and police officers. They remember why they ran for elected office or why they gave up their nights and weekends to join with their neighbors to work for a better community. Results provide a common purpose that brings people together."

Those results will serve as a guidepost as you steer your agency to success!

Steering your agency to success is about focusing on results and using data to manage performance.

Five years into our journey at DCF, we have changed the way we think about performance. Before implementing RBA, we often assessed performance based on anecdotal information, which is often incorrect and misleading. We based important decisions on what we thought we knew.

Now, program leads complete RBA report cards for their programs on a quarterly basis, work with providers to understand the story behind the baseline, and make necessary changes to improve performance to ensure our clients are better off as a result of our services.

Similarly, our agency management teams are using performance data to evaluate how they are doing, and whether their strategies are resulting in children and families being better off.

You can find some samples of our work in Appendix G: Turning Curves at the Connecticut Department of Children and Families.

We still hit occasional bumps in the road when working on our strategies and with our programs. But with RBA, we have a framework to evaluate whether we're headed in the right direction, and if necessary, change direction. It isn't always easy, and we still have to make difficult decisions and engage in new behaviors. But we are seeing improvement in our work. For us, that is the difference between spinning our wheels and using RBA to steer our agency to success.

Appendix A

Results-Based Accountability™ Terms Defined[10]

The Language of Accountability:

The most common problem in Results-Based Accountability or any similar work is the problem of language. People come to the table from many different disciplines and many different walks of life. And the way in which we talk about programs, services and populations varies all over the map. This means that the usual state of affairs in planning for children, families, adults, elders and communities is a Tower of Babel, where no one really knows what the other person is saying, but everyone politely pretends that they do. As a consequence, the work is slow, frustrating and often ineffective.

It is possible to exercise language discipline. And the way to do this is to agree on a set of definitions that start with ideas and not words. Words are just labels for ideas. And the same idea can have many different labels. The following nine ideas are central to RBA. The labels for these ideas are those chosen by the Appropriations Committee in Connecticut to ensure that everyone means the same thing when they use these ideas. They are the same terms that Mark Friedman uses in all of his material.

---

10 Connecticut General Assembly. Glossary of RBA Terms Used in Connecticut. Web. 2 February 2014 available at:
http://www.ct.gov/dcf/lib/dcf/rba/pdf/RBAGlossary-2014.pdf

Results are conditions of well-being for entire populations - children, adults, families or communities - stated in plain English, or any other language. They are things that voters and taxpayers can understand. They are not about programs or agencies or government jargon. Results include: healthy children, children ready for school, children succeeding in school, children staying out of trouble, strong families, elders living with dignity in settings they prefer, safe communities, a healthy clean environment, a prosperous economy. In Connecticut, we refer to these as population results, or quality of life results.

Indicators are measures that help quantify the achievement of a population result. They answer the question "How would we recognize these results in measurable terms if we fell over them?" So, for example, the rate of low birth weight babies helps quantify whether we're getting healthy births. Third grade reading scores help quantify whether children are succeeding in school today and whether they were ready for school three years ago. The crime rate helps quantify whether we are living in safe communities. Indicators refer only to whole populations, not programs.

Strategies are coherent collections of actions that have a reasoned chance of improving results. Strategies are made up of our best thinking about what works, and they include the contributions of many partners. No single action by any one agency can create the improved results we want and need.

Programs are specific ways of implementing strategies, usually targeted toward a specific sub-group within the population. Programs are not themselves strategies; they are expressions of strategies. For example, a family support strategy may have as one of its programs a "Nurturing Families Network", which is targeted at new parents at risk of abusing or neglecting their newborn child.

Performance Measures are measures of how well public and private programs and agencies are working. The most important performance measures tell us whether the clients or customers of the program or service are better off. Measures that track the quality of the program are also important. In Connecticut, we refer to measures of whether clients are better off as client or customer outcomes (to distinguish them from population results for all children, adults or families). Performance measure can apply to individual programs, entire agencies, or service delivery systems.

Baselines are what we call a trend line of an indicator or program measure when presented in a chart. The baseline consists of the history of the measure (what the measure has been for the last 3-5 years) and the forecast of where the measure will be in 3-5 years if we keep doing what we are doing.

Story Behind the Baseline is the diagnostic phase of RBA. It identifies the causes and forces at work behind the current level of performance for an indicator. Without a clear understanding of what is causing the performance to be the way it is, any strategies or actions are likely to be just random good ideas.

Turning the Curve describes efforts to improve the direction or rate of change in the baseline of an indicator or performance measure. It is also shorthand for the process of determining whether the current and projected level on an indicator or performance measure is acceptable or requires change. We Turn the Curve with strategies and actions that are based on:

What Works: what we know from the research, best practices, and our own experience that is likely to address the story behind the baselines.

Ends and Means are an important distinction in RBA. Results and indicators are about the ends we want for children and families. Strategies, programs, and performance measures are about the means to get there. Processes that fail to make this crucial distinction often mix up ends and means. Ends are usually something everyone can agree on, e.g., people with better health, more education, safer streets. This agreement forms a common ground that allows the discussions to focus on the means, about which there are often legitimate differences of opinion that can be explored. Failed processes tend to get mired in a mixed discussion about ends and means that causes hopeless confusion and disillusionment. Clarity and discipline about language at the start will help you take your work from talk to action.

What about **Mission and Vision, Values, Benchmarks, Goals, Objectives, Problems, Issues, Inputs and Outputs**? Many of us have grown up with these traditional words in strategic planning and budgeting. Where do they fit? Remember that words are just labels for ideas. These ten words have no natural standard definitions that bridge across all the different ways they are used. They are terms of art which can and are used to label many different ideas. This is why we pay so much attention to getting language discipline straight at the very beginning. It's the ideas that are important, not the words. To avoid confusion, Connecticut does not use these words in its RBA work. For more information on how these words can be used in other contexts, see Mark Friedman's discussion of The Language of Accountability at the footnote on page 1.

Appendix B

Text of Act Requiring an Annual Results-Based Acountability Report Card Evaluating Policies and Programs Impacting Children

Substitute House Bill No. 6282

Public Act No. 11-109

AN ACT REQUIRING AN ANNUAL RESULTS-BASED ACCOUNTABILITY REPORT CARD EVALUATING STATE POLICIES AND PROGRAMS IMPACTING CHILDREN.

Be it enacted by the Senate and House of Representatives in General Assembly convened:

Section 1. (NEW) (*Effective July 1, 2011*) (a) The select committee of the General Assembly having cognizance of matters relating to children, in consultation with the Office of Fiscal Analysis, the Office of Legislative Research and the Commission on Children, shall maintain an annual report card that evaluates the progress of state policies and programs in promoting the result that all Connecticut children grow up in a stable living environment, safe, healthy and ready to lead successful lives. Progress shall be measured by primary indicators of progress, including, but not limited to, indicators established in the final report of the Legislative Program Review and Investigations Committee prepared pursuant to the provisions of section 1 of public act 09-166, of state-wide rates of child abuse, child poverty, low birth weight, third grade reading proficiency, and the annual social health index developed pursuant to section 46a-131a of the general statutes. For each indicator, the data shall also be presented according to ethnicity or race, gender, geography and, where appropriate, age and other relevant characteristics. Said committee shall prepare the report card on or before January 15, 2012, and annually thereafter. On or before January 15, 2012, and annually thereafter, said committee shall make the report card available to the public on the Internet and on the web site of the General Assembly and shall transmit the report card electronically to (1) members of the joint standing committees of the General Assembly having cognizance of matters relating to appropriations and the budgets of state agencies and human services, (2) the Commissioners of Children and Families, Education and Public Health, (3) the Child Advocate, (4) the Secretary of the Office of Policy and Management, and (5) the Chief Court Administrator.

(b) On or before January 15, 2012, the select committee of the General Assembly having cognizance of matters relating to children, in consultation with a working group of representatives of state agencies and departments, community organizations, private provider agencies operating programs that impact the well-being of children and families, parents and other caretakers of children, child advocacy organizations, health care professionals that serve children and families, schools, and child care providers, shall identify or develop (1) an indicator for measuring whether children are living with their families and have stability in their living environments, (2) secondary indicators for measuring progress within each area of children's well-being related to measuring progress in their health, safety, stability, education and future success, including, but not limited to, food security, and (3) key measures of performance of the state child welfare system, including, but not limited to, (A) rates of repeat maltreatment among victims of child abuse and neglect; (B) placement in out-of-home care among children at risk of abuse and neglect; (C) child fatalities involving child abuse or neglect; (D) rates of reunification and permanency for children removed from their homes; and (E) the developmental and health status and educational progress of children served by the child welfare system and other appropriate measures of well-being and preparation for success in life. Not less than annually, said committee shall: (i) With the assistance of the working group, review the adequacy of primary and secondary indicators, system-level performance measures, and related data resources for such indicators and measures, and determine whether there are more appropriate alternatives to monitoring progress in achieving the result that all Connecticut children grow up in a stable living environment, safe, healthy and ready to lead successful lives, and (ii) in consultation with the results-based accountability subcommittee of the joint standing committee of the General Assembly having cognizance of matters relating to appropriations and the budgets of state agencies, identify programs within the child welfare system that make a significant contribution to achieving such result and require the entities administering such programs to prepare annual report cards employing the results-based format developed by said subcommittee.

Approved July 8, 2011

Appendix C

RBA Report Card Template

Developed by CT General Assembly, Appropriations Committee

2015 Program Report Card: [Insert Program Name (Insert Agency Name)]

Quality of Life Result (Insert Result)

Contribution to the Result (Insert Contribution)

Program Expenditures	**State Funding**	**Federal Funding**	**Other Financing**	**Total Funding**
Actual SFY 14				
Estimated SFY 15				

Partners (Insert Partners)

How Much Did We Do?
(Insert name of measure)

(Insert graph or table)

Story behind the baseline:

Trend: [Use ▲, ▼ or ▼▲]

How Well Did We Do It?
(Insert name of measure)

(Insert graph or table)

Story behind the baseline:

Trend: [Use ▲, ▼ or ▼▲]

How Well Did We Do It?
(Insert name of measure)

(Insert graph or table)

Story behind the baseline:

Trend: [Use ▲, ▼ or ▼▲]

Trend Going in Right Direction? ▲ Yes; ▼ No. ▼▲ Flat/No Trend

RBA Report Card Template *(continued)*

2015 Program Report Card: [Insert Program Name (Insert Agency Name)]

Quality of Life Result (Insert Result)

Is Anyone Better Off? *(Insert name of measure)*	**Is Anyone Better Off?** *(Insert name of measure)*	**Proposed Actions to Turn the Curve**
(Insert graph or table)	*(Insert graph or table)*	
Story behind the baseline:	**Story behind the baseline:**	**Data Development Agenda:**
Trend: [Use ▲, ▼ or ▼▲]	Trend: [Use ▲, ▼ or ▼▲]	

Trend Going in Right Direction?   ▲ Yes;   ▼ No.   ▼▲ Flat/No Trend

Appendix D

PowerPoint Presentation: Hands On! Creating your RBA Report Card

---

**Hands On!
Creating your RBA Report Card**

Developing and Using RBA Report Cards

Anne McIntyre-Lahner
May 2015

**Part I
Data and Performance Measures**

...using RBA...

- Focus on data that will tell you how kids are doing and whether anyone is better off
    - Data for the sake of data is interesting but... stay on track and get what you can use
- Disaggregate, disaggregate, disaggregate!
- What do these data tell you about the children and adolescents you are working with?
- What else do you need to know?

Performance Measure Review

- Think RBA:
- Start with the end in mind:
    - Why are you funding this service?
    - What do you hope to achieve?
    - What does success look like?
    - How will you know if the service was successful?

Identifying Headline Measures

- Identify Five Headline Measures for your report card

- 1 or 2 "How Much" measures

- 1 or 2 "How Well" measure

- 2 or 3 "Better Off" measures

- Which performance measures will you use as headline measures for your RBA Report Card?

- How much work must be done to share/understand the data?

Make sure you are telling the correct story.....and telling the story correctly

Is Truncating the Y-Axis Dishonest?

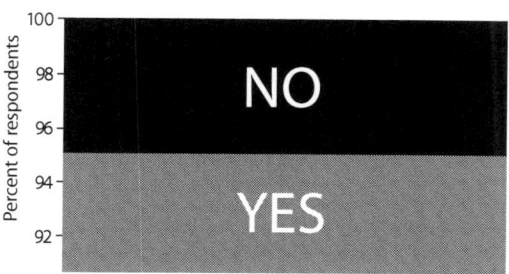

Andrew Kniss, Associate Professor, University of Wyoming, Dept of Plant Sciences

Part II
Developing the Report Card

RBA Report Cards

- Brief presentation of salient information
- Format developed by the Appropriations Committee of the Connecticut General Assembly
- Two-pages
- Use charts to effectively tell the story about performance
- When writing your story, brevity is key!
- For the story behind the baseline, DON'T describe what the data already show; tell the story about WHY the data are what they are
- Identify what you will do to improve performance
- Identify additional data needed to best understand performance

The Report Card Template

2015 DCF Program Report Card: [Insert Program Name (Insert Agency Name)]

Quality of Life Result (Insert Result)
Contribution to the Result (Insert Contribution)

Program Expenditures	State Funding	Federal Funding	Other Financing	Total Funding
Actual SFY 14				
Estimated SFY 15				

Partners (Insert Partners)

How Much Did We Do?	How Well Did We Do It?	How Much Did We Do?
(Insert name of measure)	*(Insert name of measure)*	*(Insert name of measure)*
(Insert graph or table)	*(Insert graph or table)*	*(Insert graph or table)*
Story behind the baseline:	**Story behind the baseline:**	**Story behind the baseline:**
Trend: [Use ▲, ▼ or ◄►]	Trend: [Use ▲, ▼ or ◄►]	Trend: [Use ▲, ▼ or ◄►]

Trend Going in Right Direction?   ▲ Yes; ▼ No.   ◄► Flat/No Trend

2015 DCF Program Report Card: [Insert Program Name (Insert Agency Name)]

Quality of Life Result (Insert Result)

Is Anyone Better Off?	Is Anyone Better Off?	Proposed Actions to Turn the Curve
(Insert name of measure)	*(Insert name of measure)*	
(Insert graph or table)	*(Insert graph or table)*	Data Development Agenda:
Story behind the baseline:	Story behind the baseline:	
Trend: [Use ▲, ▼ or ◄ ►]	Trend: [Use ▲, ▼ or ◄ ►]	

Trend Going in Right Direction?   ▲ Yes; ▼ No.   ◄ ► Flat/No Trend

Sections of the Report Card

Quality of Life Result

- Population Level Result:
  - Connecticut children grow up stable environments, safe, healthy, and ready to lead successful lives.
  - All Connecticut working age residents have jobs that provide financial self-sufficiency

- Describe the program's contribution to the population level result. This section should summarize the most important contributions to the population level result.

Program Expenditures

Program Expenditures	State Funding	Federal Funding	Other Funding	Total Funding
Actual SFY 15				
Estimated SFY 15				

Partners

- Identify the major internal and external partners needed for the program to succeed

- Internal partners are divisions, regions, facilities, or colleagues within DCF that you can work with to implement the program

- External partners are people outside DCF (including families, other agencies, and contracted providers) that you can engage to better implement the program

How Much Did We Do?

How Much Did We Do?
(Insert name of measure)

(Insert graph or table)

Story behind the baseline:

Trend: [Use ▲, ▼ or ◄►]

How Much Did We Do?
The number of children placed in TFC Homes

Story behind the baseline:
The above trend in data is reflective of the department's initiative to decrease reliance on congregate care, both in and out of state. The data for this fiscal year shows a steady increase in admissions to TFC programs of 50 children and youth over the three quarters.
Trend: ▲

How Well Did We Do It?

How Well Did We Do It?

(Insert name of measure)

(Insert graph or table)

Story behind the baseline:

Trend: [Use ▲, ▼ or ◄►]

How Well Did We Do It?

Performance Measure 2: Percentage of active clients who participated in a Youth Business Program, Internship, were Employed or attending a Post-Secondary Educational or Vocational program

Participation in Workforce Readiness Activities

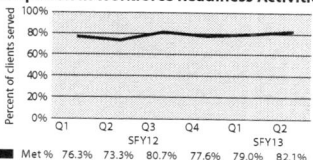

	Q1	Q2	Q3	Q4	Q1	Q2
	SFY12				SFY13	
Met %	76.3%	73.3%	80.7%	77.6%	79.0%	82.1%
Met #	225	222	205	208	252	215

Story behind the Baseline:
A majority of clients have performed well on this measure, with the percentage steadily increasing from 73.3% in Q4 2011 to 82.1% in Q1 2013. This is notable given that a percentage of this population may not be ready for a work experience (i.e. under age 16, or working through mental health issues), or may be engaged in other activities, such as sports, that compete for their free time. Providers have worked closely with the area offices to maintain this trend. The 17.9% of clients who do not show up in the data as "engaged" may be the population that is under 16 and in school. We have identified this for the data development agenda

Trend: ▲

Is Anyone Better Off?

Is Anyone Better Off?

(Insert name of measure)

(Insert graph or table)

Story behind the baseline:

Trend: [Use ▲, ▼ or ◄►]

Is Anyone Better Off?

Percent of children not suspended or expelled following participation

At-Risk Children Not Suspended-Expelled

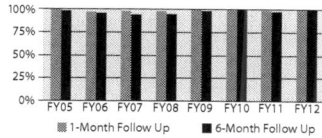

■ 1-Month Follow Up   ■ 6-Month Follow Up

Story behind the baseline:
The preschool expulsion rate in CT was 12.48 per every 1000 children, the 9th highest rating in the country (Gilliam 2005). Children are referred to ECCP because they are at risk of suspension-expulsion. At 1 month follow-up, an average of 99% of children who received ECCP services were not suspended/expelled from their early care and education setting. At 6 month follow-up, an average of 97% were not suspended or expelled. The chart above represents a breakdown of percentages by fiscal year where 1 and 6 month follow up data were available.
Trend: ▲

Story Behind the Baseline

- List briefly, in bullet format and in order of priority, the most important factors that influence the slope of the trend line (the "curve") for the data for each headline measure.

  - positive and negative,
  - current and anticipated

- This is not a re-statement of the data, but a discussion about what factors are impacting the data.

Proposed Actions to Turn the Curve

- Based on the performance you are reporting, and the story behind the baseline, identify the actions you will take to improve performance.

- Example:

  - The DCF program lead will work with the provider to assure that the Contractor case managers are better qualified to provide families education on the financial management and to assist families in accessing vocational and employment programs in the community

Data Development and Research Agenda

- Identify data which would empower you to better manage performance but you do not currently have.

- Example

  Levels of Service Categories will be reevaluated for more precise analysis of service need, and increased accuracy with utilization reporting;

  Increased capacity is needed to understand why some clients are not showing up in the system as "engaged." and the reasons and barriers that may exist.

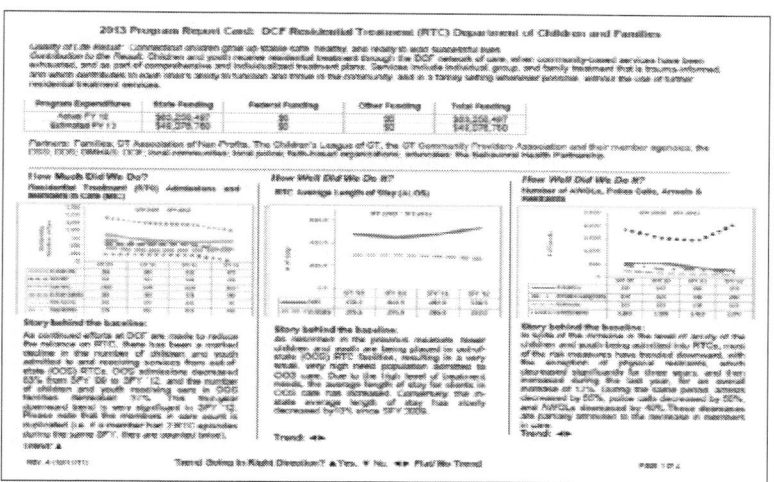

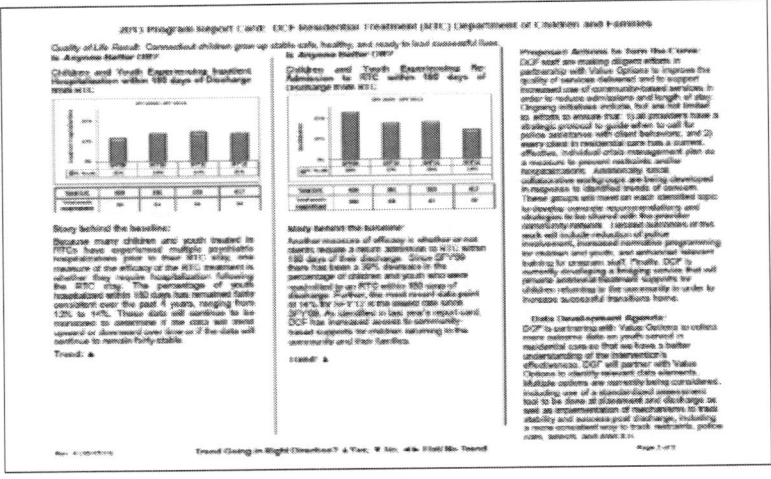

What you can learn from your report card

- If you use the data on an ongoing basis, you'll be able to measure where you're doing something right.

- If you aren't getting desired outcomes, look at performance data

- When you find you are doing something wrong, say it:

    We're doing something wrong ...
    what do we need to do differently?

So What Do We Do To Improve Performance?

- Work with your provider to understand performance by using your performance data

- Determine where improvement can be achieved

- Agree on how the provider can improve performance and where you may be able to assist

- Repeat

- Repeat

- Repeat

Using RBA Report Cards to Inform

- Reporting performance to the DCF Service Array Review team

- **Opportunity to learn about how we are doing and Whether anyone is better off**

- Opportunity to acknowledge good performance

- Opportunity to identify strategies to improve performance
  - Provider performance
  - Appropriateness of program model
  - Partner with regions and other divisions

Appendix E

PowerPoint Presentation: Introduction to Using Results-Based Accountability to Strengthen Services for the Well-being of Connecticut's Kids

Using Results Based Accountability to Strengthen Services for the Well-being of Connecticut's Kids:

Developing Performance Measures

Anne McIntyre-Lahner
Director of Performance Management
Connecticut Department of Children and Families
June 22, 2015

Rule#1
Start with the end in mind.

The End.

(Just Kidding...but not really)

The 7 Performance Accountability Questions

➜ 1. Who are our customers?

➜ 2. How can we measure if our customers are better off?

➜ 3. How can we measure if we are delivering services well?

➜ 4. How are we doing on the most important of these measures?

➜ 5. Who are the partners that have a role to play in doing better?

➜ 6. What works to do better, including no-cost and low-cost ideas?

➜ 7. What do we propose to do?

Source: M. Friedman; *Trying Hard Is Not Good Enough*

DCF's Experience

DCF's RBA Performance Measure Development

■ Develop proposed performance measures:
- How much did we do?
- How well did we do it?
- Is anyone better off?

■ Develop items for exclusion:
- What can providers stop reporting?
- Model components or contract compliance items that should not be confused with outcomes

■ Identification of data sources
- Who will collect the data, and how?
- Who will report the data; how and how often?
- Who will analyze the data, and how will it be used?

DCF's Ongoing work plan to include RBA performance measures in all contracts

■ System-Wide Implementation
- All New Programs
- All Re-designed Programs
- All Re-procured Programs
- All Contracts through prioritized schedule
    ■ Service types prioritized as high, medium, or lower
    ■ Services assessed for readiness: 1, 2, or 3
- Approximately 85% of program types have RBA performance measures completed or in development

Developing Performance Measures

3 Kinds of Performance Measures

■ How much did we do?

■ How well did we do it?

■ Is anyone better off?

...3 Kinds of Performance Measures

■ How much did we do?
  - The quantity of service provided
  - This is about the quantity of work we (or our provider) performed
■ Examples:
  ■ The number of clients admitted for service
  ■ The number of trainings delivered
  ■ The number of screenings performed

...3 Kinds of Performance Measures

- How well did we do it?
  - The quality of the service provided
  - This is about the quality of work we (or our provider) performed

- Examples:
  - The percent of clients who completed service
  - The amount of time from admission to first appointment
  - The percent of clients who report they feel respected by the provider

...3 Kinds of Performance Measures

- Is anyone better off?
  - The outcome for the client
  - This is about how the client is better off after our service

- 4 Types of "better off" measures
  - Change in skills/knowledge
  - Change in attitude
  - Change in behavior
  - Change in circumstance

......is anyone better off?

- Examples:
  - The percent of clients who increased their subject matter knowledge
  - The percent of clients who graduated/were promoted to the next grade
  - The percent of clients who are clean and sober
  - The percent of clients who report a change in feelings about hope for the future
  - The percent of clients who have stable and affordable housing

Developing Performance Measures

- Think RBA:

- Start with the end in mind:
  - Why are you funding this service?
  - What do you hope to achieve?
  - What does success look like?
  - How will you know if the service was successful?

... Developing Performance Measures

■ What does success look like for your clients?

■ What are the specific services/deliverables that will lead to client success?

■ What is reasonable to expect through this contract?

...Developing Performance Measures

■ How will you measure the amount of work performed?
  - (How much will we do?)

■ How will you know if the provider has done a good job?
  - (How will we know how well we do?)

■ How will you know if your provider has made a difference for your clients?
  - (How will we know if anyone is better off?)

The Data

■ What data will you use to report performance?

■ Do the data exist now?

■ Who has access to the data?

■ How much work must be done to share/understand the data?

Ensuring the right level of Accountability

■ Make sure the desired "Better Off" measure can be reasonably connected to the program elements

■ Make sure performance measures are appropriately aligned to the actual service

■ Make sure the identified performance is within the provider's control

Summary

- Start with the end in mind: why are you funding/delivering this service?
- Know how you will utilize performance measures and outcome data
- Use of performance measures and outcomes to manage performance
  - -Make sure you are measuring the right things
  - -use data to understand program performance
  - -don't be surprised by your RBA Report Card
- Program Leads (PDOCs)
- Program leads need training and support in order to support provider partners and to manage contracts

Closing thought

- Overwhelmed?

- New to RBA?

- Have to work with non-believers?

- Afraid to get it wrong?

Remember........

Great Ideas

***Nothing will ever be
attempted if all
possible objections
must first be overcome***

***Samuel Johnson
1709 - 1784, British Author***

Appendix F

Governor's Cabinet on Nonprofit Health and Human Services Population Results Work Group Recommendations
(October 30, 2013)

Contents

Introduction 1

Summary of Objectives and Recommendations 2

Appendix A. Lessons Learned: A Guide for
Connecting Population Results and Performance
Measures in Purchase of Service Contracts 4

Appendix B. Headline Indicators by Result
and Data Source 12

Introduction

The Governor's Cabinet on Nonprofit Health and Human Services Population Results Work Group was given the charge of building on the work of last year's group and providing recommendations to the Governor on incorporation of performance measures that demonstrate the contribution of the program to population results into Purchase of Services contracts for health and human services.

The Work Group members are:

Yvette Bello, Latino Community Services, Co-Chair
Ajit Gopalakrishnan, SDE, Co-Chair

Roderick Bremby, DSS
Rhonda Evans, CT Assoc. for Community Action
Karin Haberlin, DMHAS
Susan Keane, Appropriations Committee
Karl Lewis, DOC
Anne McIntyre-Lahner, DCF
Cynthia McKenna, Catholic Charities
Rick Porth, United Way
Bennett Pudlin, Charter Oak Group
Nancy Roberts, CT Council of Philanthropy

Summary of Objectives and Recommendations

Objective	Work Completed	Recommendations
Explore and document existing process and practices within government, nonprofit, and philanthropic entities for connecting population results to outcome measures within service contracts.	Presentations to work group by Departments of Children and Families (DCF) and Mental Health and Addiction Services (DMHAS), Court Support Services Division (CSSD) and United Way on how their agencies have incorporated population indicators and performance measures into purchase of service (POS)contracts	**Recommendation 1**: Performance measures within purchase of service (POS) contracts for health and human services should demonstrate a program's contribution to population indicators and results. To ensure the consistent incorporation of such performance measures into POS contracts across all state agencies and branches of state government and to avoid subjecting providers to differing requirements, it is recommended that the Executive Branch, in consultation with the Legislative Branch and Judicial Branch, establish a policy-level coordinating entity to lead this effort. **Recommendation 2**: Any state agency that awards health and human services POS contracts is strongly encouraged to establish an intra-agency team (that includes staff from data, operations, and contracts divisions) to support the inclusion of appropriate performance measures into POS contracts. **Recommendation 3**: State agencies, funders and providers need adequate support to develop, implement and use appropriate performance measures as outlined in Recommendations 1 and 2. Therefore, it is recommended that the coordinating entity arrange for the provision of adequate support from experts in this area. It is further recommended that the document created by the Population Results work group entitled *Lessons Learned: A Guide for Connecting Population Results and Performance Measures in Purchase of Service Contracts* (Appendix A) be used to guide this work. *(continued on page 108)*

Summary of Objectives and Recommendations (*continued*)

Objective	Work Completed	Recommendations
Refine the list of population indicators and finalize for adoption by Cabinet	Building on last year's work, the Work Group on Population Results began to vet the population indicators in the various domains and determined that indicators need to be populated with data for additional vetting. Support from OPM was offered and accepted and a list of state agency contacts with access to the data has been developed. In addition, the indicators from the CTKIDS Report Card of the CT General Assembly, Committee on Children, that were adopted last year by the Cabinet, are included. Appendix B represents the entire list of indicators.	**Recommendation 4:** The preliminary population indicators elected by the 2011-12 work group (see Appendix B) should be refined by the work group referenced in Recommendation 6 using actual data, and this process of refinement should be an ongoing one.
Recommend a structure for organizing and maintaining population indicators and support for application of framework	Presentations by CTdata.org Weave platform and the CT State Data Center	**Recommendation 5:** CTdata.org, managed by the CT Data Collaborative, is the recommended structure to acquire, maintain and make accessible the population indicators. **Recommendation 6:** A work group similar in composition to the current Population Results Work Group of the Cabinet that is broadly representative of all stakeholders including all branches of government, funders and providers, should be established to advise the coordinating entity on the work encompassed in Recommendations 1 through 5. Governor's Cabinet on Nonprofit Health and Human Services

Appendix A.

Lessons Learned: A Guide for Connecting Population Results and Performance Measures in Purchase of Service Contracts

Contents

I. FLOWCHART FOR CONNECTING POPULATION RESULTS AND PERFORMANCE MEASURES

II. INTRODUCTION

III. DEVELOPING RESULTS, INDICATORS, AND PERFORMANCE MEASURES

IV. USING RESULTS, INDICATORS, AND PERFORMANCE MEASURES TO TURN THE CURVE

I. FLOWCHART FOR CONNECTING POPULATION RESULTS AND PERFORMANCE MEASURES

This Guide is offered as a way to tie program performance measures (performance accountability), particularly client outcomes, to population level results (population accountability) by selecting and using measures that are most meaningful for program management and improvement and that help illustrate the program's contribution to the result, while at the same time making clear the program's appropriate level of accountability.

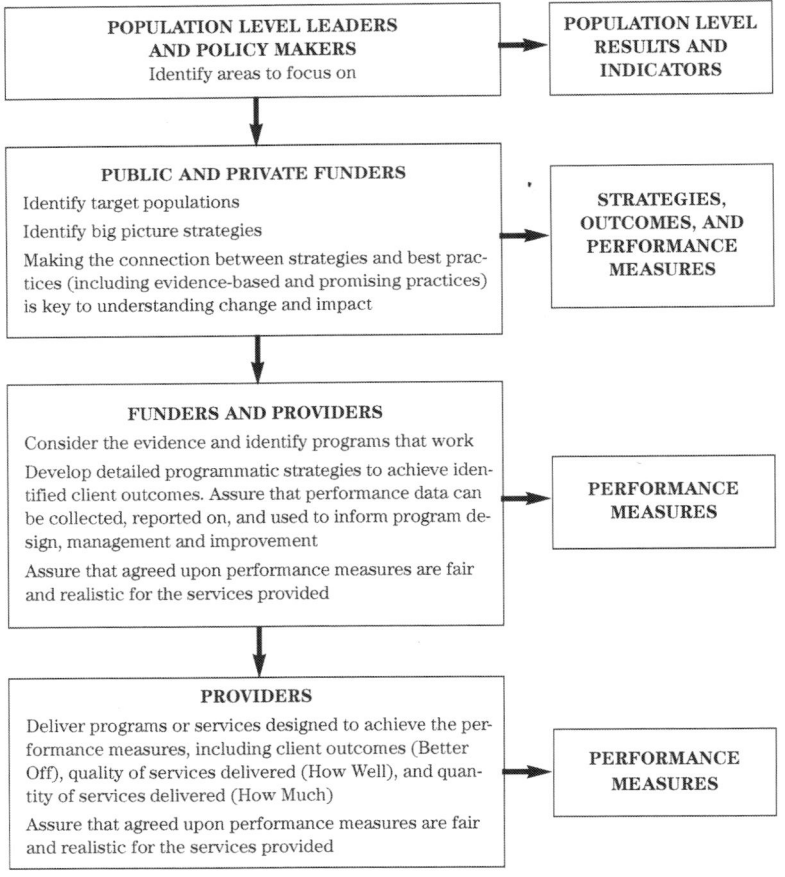

Governor's Cabinet on Nonprofit Health and Human Services
Population Results Work Group Recommendations, October 30, 2013

110

II. Introduction

Funders are increasingly embracing performance measurement as a way to ensure that taxpayer and donor dollars are well spent and to improve program quality. However, the best run program is only of actual value when the program contributes to a desired result. Programs are means to an end, and funders and policy makers should be interested in programs primarily based on how they contribute to a population level, quality of life result.

This Guide is offered as a way to tie program performance measures (performance accountability), particularly client outcomes, to population level results (population accountability) by selecting and using measures that are most meaningful for program management and improvement and that help illustrate the program's contribution to the result, while at the same time making clear the program's appropriate level of accountability.

To ensure that we keep the distinction between population accountability and performance accountability, we need clarity about the language we use. The Appropriations Committee of Connecticut General Assembly has adopted the following language for use by Connecticut state agencies:

Results are conditions of well-being for entire populations — children, adults, families or communities — stated in plain English, or any other language. They are things that voters and taxpayers can understand. They are not about programs or agencies or government jargon.

Indicators are measures that help quantify the achievement of a population result. They answer the question "How would we recognize these results in measurable terms if we fell over them?"

Performance Measures are measures of how well public and private programs and agencies are working. The most important performance measures tell us whether the clients or customers of the program's service are better off. Measures that track the quality of the program, including the extent to which it reaches the intended beneficiaries, are also important.

Story Behind the Baseline is the diagnostic phase of this work. It identifies the causes and forces at work behind the current level of performance for an indicator or performance measure. Without a clear understanding of what is causing the performance to be the way it is, any strategies or actions are likely to be just random good ideas.[1]

This Guide is based on the following principles:

No one program or agency can be held responsible for population results or large systems change.

Accountability is important, and because of that, funders have the responsibility to require performance measures. This is where the alignment between program performance and population results is most important. From the program's perspective, this is a way in which providers get to show the contribution of the program and its alignment with critical agency/funder strategies.

Funders and providers are partners in this work and hold complementary and interdependent roles in contributing to

---

1 Connecticut RBA Glossary, based on the work of Mark Friedman, found online at: http://www.cga.ct.gov/app/rba/2013/CT%20RBA%20Glossary%20Rev%20%201%20(12%2031%2011).pdf

population level results (and the client outcomes that contribute to those results). The process for developing and implementing performance measures should be reflective of this relationship between and among the various partners.

Lack of desired outcomes does not necessarily mean that a program, a provider, or a service design has failed; rather, the story behind the data must be understood in order to inform next steps. Less than optimal performance, especially on client outcomes, will signal the partners to first understand the story behind the data and to identify areas for improvement.

State agencies need both support from the state budget office and control agencies, and a degree of autonomy in working out performance contracts with their providers; the old approach to contracting that keeps providers at arm's length until a contract is signed is not conducive to the kinds of partnership that are required for achieving population results.

III. DEVELOPING RESULTS, INDICATORS AND PERFORMANCE MEASURES

A. Overlapping Roles and Responsibilities

Population level leaders and policy makers:

Responsible for identifying population level result statements and indicators; assigning responsibility for populating and maintaining the indicators; using the analysis of the data and the relevant research to specify areas of strategic focus and high level strategies.

State budget office and control agencies:

Responsible for building a foundation for state agency contracting processes; providing a common framework for performance measure development; and providing support to state agencies and nonprofit organizations in the development and use of performance measures.

State agencies and funders:

Responsible for convening work groups to analyze the data, examine the research and evidence base, determine best practices, and develop high-level/big picture strategies to achieve desired outcomes for the entire population or identified portions of the population/targeted client groups.

Contracting units, program leads, program developers

Responsible for convening agency and provider teams to jointly develop detailed agency and programmatic strategies with performance measures, including client outcomes.

Program operators and community providers:

Responsible for developing and delivering programs, initiatives, and services that are designed to achieve client outcomes and for reporting performance measures that have been jointly developed by providers, public agencies, and private funders.

B. Lessons Learned from Early Impleme nter Agencies and Funders

1. **Institutionalizing performance accountability** within the state/funding agency **and building organizational and staff capacity** before measuring provider performance will help to ensure a successful rollout of performance measures in POS contracts.

The Judicial Branch - Court Support Services Division (CSSD) developed a reporting system and performance measures for internal use and trained its staff before including these measures in POS contracts. Performance measures were developed and utilized to manage state employee (e.g. probation officer) performance at least three years prior to inclusion in POS contracts.

DCF developed its strategic plan using Results-Based Accountability (RBA), and sent a team of staff members to advanced RBA training to assist with strategic planning and performance measure development across the agency.

DMHAS has based many key performance measures on the National Outcome Measures developed and required by the Substance Abuse and Mental Health Services Administration (SAMHSA). These measures, as well as other system measures developed by DMHAS, have been incorporated into provider quality reports. DMHAS plans to begin publishing these provider quality reports on its public website starting in December 2013.

United Way identified a set of national strategic priorities based on population-level indicators and an understanding of what works to impact client outcomes. The United Way priorities will be used to develop outcome-based grants and contracts that are aligned to these indicators.

2. When developing performance measures, state/funding agencies should **start with the ends they are seeking** and then ensure that the means are appropriate. Can the service in question reasonably and realistically be ex-

pected to achieve these ends? Specifically, ask the following questions:

What is the population result to which this service makes the greatest contribution?

What is the purpose of this program? Why is this service being funded; what do we hope to achieve by implementing this service?

Through what services and activities does this program actually contribute to the result?

What performance measures do we need in order to understand the quality of the program and its impact on its clients?

- HOW MUCH: How can we measure how many clients we are serving and services we are delivering?

- HOW WELL: How will we know if we are doing a good job of reaching the target population and delivering services well?

- BETTER OFF: How will we know that clients/customers are better off for having participating in this program?

3. State/funding agencies need to **involve providers** at the earliest possible stage of performance measure development and selection.

CSSD engaged Connecticut Community Providers Association and Connecticut Association of Nonprofits to convene performance measure development meetings between CSSD and provider agencies. The purpose of these meetings was to clarify the desired population result, achieve consensus on program performance measures, and agree to an implementation plan and timeline. These groups meet regularly to monitor the process.

DCF program leads met with providers to jointly develop performance measures across program types. DCF has learned that it is important to involve providers on at least three different levels: provider agency staff from multiple levels within individual agencies; provider agency staff, across multiple agencies, by program type; and provider trade groups.

DMHAS convenes regular bi-monthly conference calls with its funded providers to discuss data quality and performance measures. Additionally, after each new quarterly provider quality report release, DMHAS holds provider forums to review results and receive feedback. This process has been ongoing since 2009.

Several United Way organizations in Connecticut request that grantees initially identify performance measures in their proposals for funding and explain how the proposed program will contribute to the results United Way has identified. Upon an award, grantees are then required to engage in the development of common performance measures with other grantees working on programs that contribute to the same result.

4. Before committing to a set of performance measure for POS contracts, the state/funding agency and provider partners need to **develop measures that are meaningful, reliable, and valid** and that, ideally, have been tested,

tweaked over time, and piloted. Identifying data sources is an important step in this process. Good performance measures cannot be developed without good data. The involvement of the providers does not stop with the selection of the measures but must include the "operationalization" of the measures, the process by which technical aspects of the measure are refined and data are collected and reported.

CSSD worked for years to build its data system and capacity before embarking on this project. In 2003 and 2005, CSSD launched a completely redesigned Case Management Information System that would serve as the foundation for performance measurement of its internal programs. In 2007, it launched the Contractor Data Collection System, which would become the hub of data for contractor performance measurement.

DCF piloted training and a set of tools to help program leads and providers develop performance measures that measure the quantity and quality of contracted work and anticipated client outcomes. The pilot helped DCF learn the importance of also identifying data availability and sources as a key part of the process.

DMHAS maintains a continuous quality improvement process wherein providers and other key stakeholders review and give feedback with each quarterly provider report. Provider review of the DMHAS quality reports is essential, not only so that they may benefit from the data, but also to identify potential problems with data quality or current operationalization. However, many of DMHAS' performance measures are federally required and are not able to be modified. A number of United Ways consult with grantees to jointly determine the most appropriate performance measures based on grantee experience and United Waygoals.

5. **Separate contract compliance and fiscal accountability** from the provider performance system; they are very important but will dilute the focus on performance measures if not addressed separately. If compliance issues are included, acknowledge them as relating to the quality of service delivery (How Well), not client outcomes (Better Off).

CSSD only includes program performance measures in its performance based contracting initiative at this point. Contract compliance and fiscal accountability data collection and quality are currently being assessed. Inclusion of these two areas as performance measures in the contracting initiative will be at the "How Well" level of performance measurement only.

DCF developed a contract compliance section for POS contracts to measure and account for important service components like staffing levels, hours of operation, and certain requirements for evidence-based services, which are very important but are not necessarily performance measures.

DMHAS is exploring ways to incorporate program performance measures, standardized by level of care, into provider contracts; however, benchmarks are still being piloted as of early FY14.

IV. USING RESULTS, INDICATORS AND PERFORMANCE MEASURES TO TURN THE CURVE

A. Using Performance Measures to Manage Performance

Ideally, funders and providers **jointly analyze the data** to determine what is working well (and might be a best practice) and what requires improvement. This partnership is essential for program management and improvement and requires a degree of trust among the partners.

It is important to **develop a solid baseline of performance data** so that funders and provider partners understand the performance history in order to thoroughly investigate external factors that could be affecting individual provider performance, e.g., case load mix, regional economic conditions, demographics, local policies or systems; where appropriate, these factors need to be accounted for in the measurement approach or in any targets.

Do not introduce targets for performance measures **until** you have a **strong comfort level with the measures** and enough of a baseline to have a defensible basis for the targets. Providers need to be involved in this process for it to have credibility.

B. Supporting Strong Performance

State/funding agencies should **develop both financial and less tangible incentives** that can be provided for good performance. It is important to make sure that incentives do not create unintended consequences. For example, performance measures for an employment and training program that include employment outcomes (Better Off) could lead the program to enroll participants who were most likely to get a job even without the program. Counter-balancing the employment outcome measures with "How Well" measures that count the percent of participants who are hardest to serve eliminates the incentive to cream.

CSSD has developed the following incentives for its contracted programs:

- Letter of recognition from Judicial/CSSD
- Reduction in contract monitoring level
- Small tokens of recognition
- Staff Development / Appreciation Day (program closes for one day during Judge's Institute)

C. Addressing Under-Performing Efforts

State/funding agencies should **develop a graduated response to weak performance**. The graduated response should include a series of steps starting with funders and providers working together to first understand performance measure data and the context in which programs are operating. CSSD has developed the following steps when accountability for performance, in fact, sits with providers:

- Increase in contract monitoring
- Comprehensive program review by CSSD contracts staff
- Conditional contract
- 90-day notice of contract termination

STOP SPINNING YOUR WHEELS

The fourth and final step in the graduated response is only to be undertaken after all previous steps have been thoroughly pursued. However, all graduated responses focus on program improvement.

D. Learning From Past Performance

- Use provider past performance as part of evaluation criteria for new RFPs
- Work with vendor community to agree on what aspects of past performance are scored, how much weight each measure gets, and what percent of total score past performance accounts for.

Appendix B.

Headline Indicators by Result and Data Source

Result 1 - Economic Security: All Connecticut residents are economically secure.

Result 2 - Health: All Connecticut residents are developmentally, physically, and mentally healthy across the life span.

Result 3 - Education: All Connecticut residents succeed in education and are prepared for careers, citizenship and life.

Result 4 - Safety: All Connecticut residents live in safe families and communities.

Result 5 - CTKIDS: - All Connecticut children grow up in a stable living environment, safe, healthy and ready to lead successful lives.

Result 6 - Elderly or Disabled: All Connecticut residents who are elderly (65 +) or have disabilities live engaged lives in supportive environments of their choosing. (Indicators are included within the other results).

#	Result	Topic Description	Specific indicator(s) specified by Cross-Agency Population Results Subcommittee	Department
1	Economic Security	Unemployment Rate	Unemployed for >6 & >12 mos	CTDOL
2		Low Income Population	<200% FPL by age	Census/DSS
3		Public Assistance Recipients	Food stamp recipients	DSS
4		Employment Rate for Elderly and Disabled	% elderly or disabled who are employed	Census, DSS
5		Housing Cost Burden	% Owners/Renters paying 30/50% income to housing	DECD/DOH
6		Skilled Workforce	% Adults with some college or above or w HS diploma (Economic Security)	Census/SDE
7	Education	Ready for Kindergarten	% entering K needing instructional support (SDE)	SDE
8		3rd or 4th Grade CMT Scores	% at or above goal on CMT Reading & Math	SDE
9		High School Graduation Rate	Cohort Graduation Rate overall & Grad rate for disabled (Support for Elderly/Disabled)	SDE
10		Disconnected Youth	% 16-24 employed, in school, or in military	SDE
11		Educational Attainment	% population age 25-34 with college degree (Educational Success)	Census, Board of Regents/Higher Ed
12		College Graduation Rate	Graduation rate for HS & CT colleges \ for disabled (Support for Elderly/Disabled)	Board of Regents/ Higher Ed

#	Result	Topic Description	Specific indicator(s) specified by Cross-Agency Population Results Subcommittee	Department
13		Access to Care	% residents without health insurance	Census
14		Premature Mortality	Premature mortality (all causes <75) or % living to 75	DPH
15	Health	Mental Health	% adults and children reporting mental health less than good in past 30 days	DMHAS
16		Birth Outcomes	Low and very low birth weight	DPH
17		Obesity Rate	% residents who are obese by age	DPH (BRFSS survey)
18		Care facilities for elderly & disabled	% elderly or disabled who receive care in home based vs institutional setting	DSS has at least partial data on this
19		Crime Rate	Crime Rate, Juvenile, violent and property	DESPP
20		Family and Domestic Violence	Arrests for DV	Judicial
21	Safety	Child Welfare	Substantiated abuse & neglect	DCF
22		Abuse and Neglect of elderly & disabled	Substantiated abuse & neglect	OPA, Department on Aging
23		Traffic Crashes	Traffic crash injury or death per capita	DOT
24		School Safety	% of High School Students who felt unsafe in the past 30 days	DPH (YRBS)

125

Indicators from the CTKIDS Report Card of the CT General Assembly, Committee on Children

#			
25	Stable	Children chronically absent from school (%)	SDE
26		Families spend over 30% of income for rent (%)	ACS/KidsCount - CTData
27		No parent has full-time employment (%)	ACS - CTData
28		Families without enough money to buy food (%)	FRAC/End Hunger CT
29	Safe	Child abuse and neglect cases (per 1,000)	DCF
30		Unexpected deaths all causes ages 0-18 (#)	CT Office of Child Advocate
31		Referrals to Juvenile Court for delinquency (#)	CT Judicial Branch, Court Operations
32	Healthy	ER visits for injuries all causes ages 0-19 (per 100,000)	DPH (CHIME data)
33		Babies born with low birth weight (%)	DPH
34		Children with health insurance (%)	ACS/Census
35		Children who are obese (%)	DPH (BRFSS survey)
36	Future Success	High school students who seriously considered suicide in the past 12 months (%)	DPH (CSHS-YRBS)
37		3rd graders reading at or above state goal	SDE
38		Kindergartners needing substantial instructional support (%)	SDE
39		On-time high school graduation (%)	SDE
		Children living in poverty/households below 100% of the Federal Poverty Line (%)	ACS - CTData

Governor's Cabinet on Nonprofit Health and Human Services

Appendix G: Turning Curves at Connecticut Department of Children and Families: How Much; How Well; and Better Off Measures

Contracted Services

Caregiver Support Teams

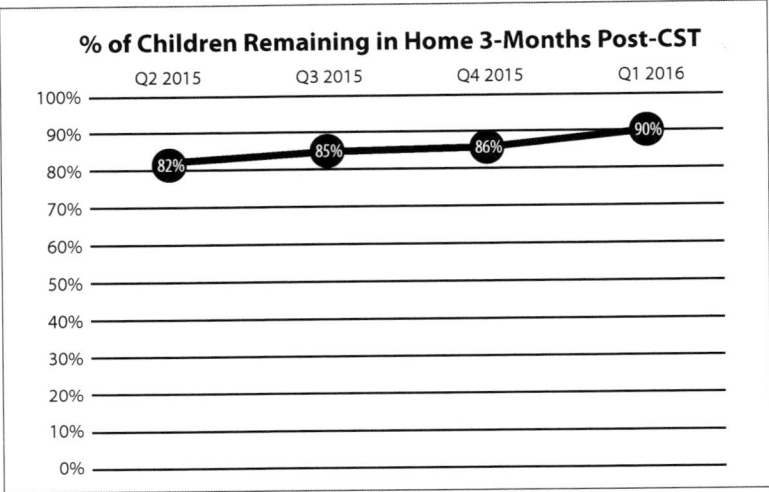

Story Behind the Baseline

Quarterly meetings with providers focused on the need for CST teams to be as involved as possible with all families' aftercare programs for at least three months. Additionally, CST team members attended many DCF and family meetings to talk about family dynamics and services needed by families. The focus on serving all families was a collaborative effort between the CST providers, the caregivers, and DCF staff.

Information developed by Brian Faraci, Program Lead

Multi-Systemic Therapy (MST)

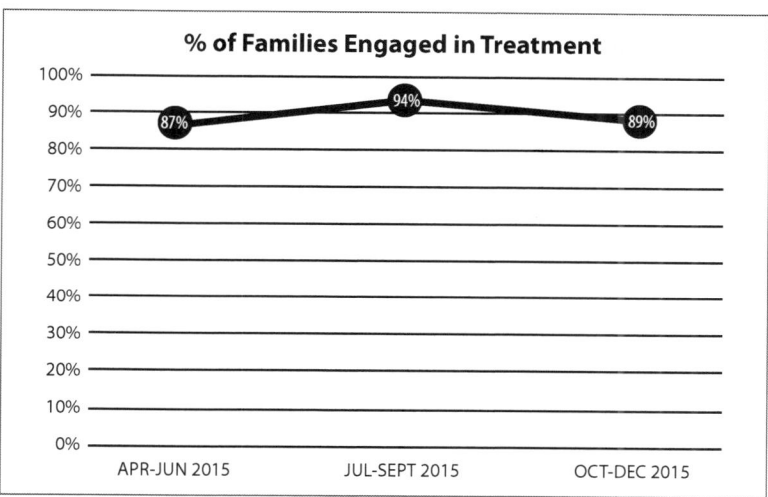

Story Behind the Baseline:

Engagement is defined as families meeting with therapists and receiving a full dose of treatment. Therapists receive weekly consultation with the MST Expert in order to improve the effectiveness of service delivery and ensure model fidelity. The consistently high performance demonstrated in this chart is reflective of the high quality family engagement and treatment service provided.

Information developed by Ines Eaton, Program Lead

High Risk Infant Program

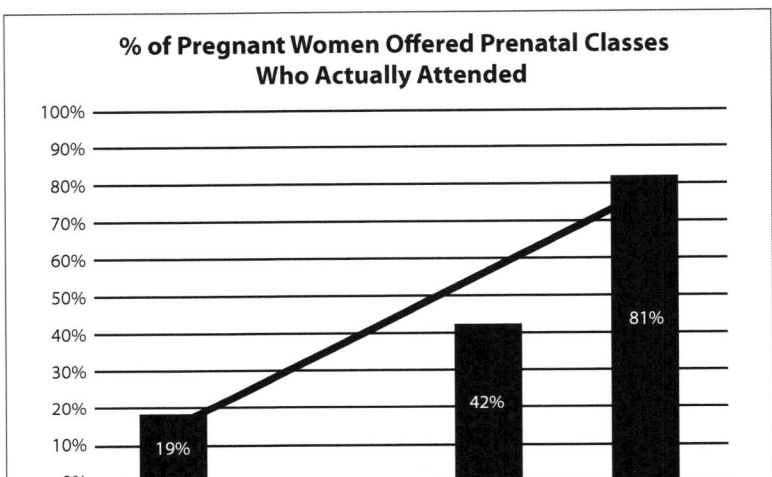

% of Pregnant Women Offered Prenatal Classes Who Actually Attended

Story behind the baseline:

A new case manager and educational instructor were hired in the 3rd quarter. The data shows a significant increase in utilization and implementation of services since that time. The newly hired case manager has demonstrated an ability to implement the program as designed, thus increasing the number of infants placed with family members as arranged by the mother. The new educational instructor has increased class attendance by connecting and navigating the prison system (clear consistent, predictable classes) and building positive relationships with the prison staff and administration.

Information developed by Dayna Snell, Program Lead

Family and Community Ties Foster Care (FaCT)

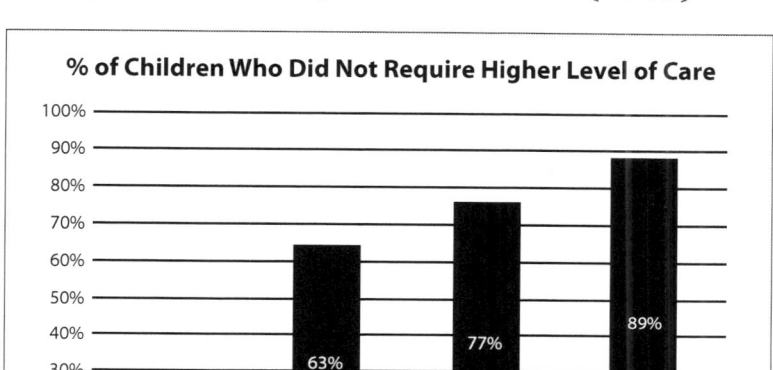

% of Children Who Did Not Require Higher Level of Care

Story behind the Baseline:

There has been a significant decline in children who require a higher level of care (i.e. psychiatric hosp., group home, etc.) since the program's inception in 2013. As foster parents and the agencies have become more seasoned, they have developed a higher tolerance for disruptive behaviors; children who were used to acting out and being placed in hospital or congregate care settings have become accustomed to living with families. With increased FaCT placements, this is significant in that it shows the capability of the program to meet the complex needs of the children and youth being served.

Information developed by Jennifer Sisk, Program Lead

Sibling Connections Camp

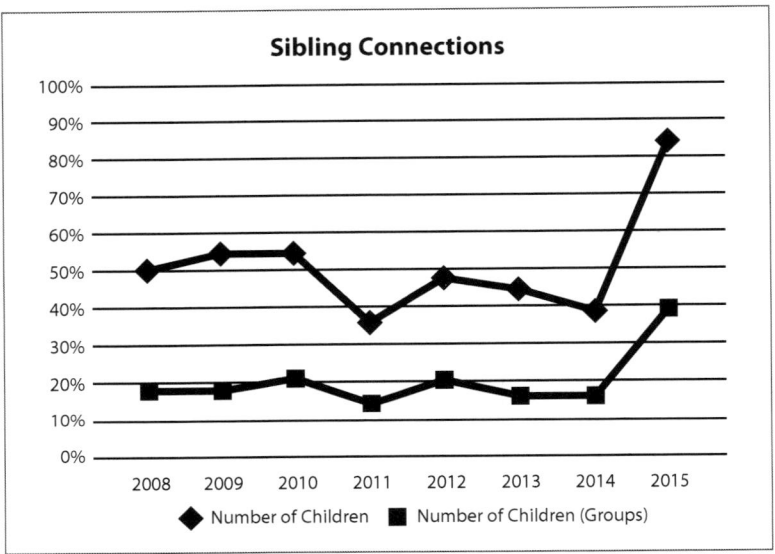

Story behind the baseline:

Until 2015, Kids Camp staff were unable to effectively recruit campers. Recruitment was performed exclusively by staff, and the date of the camp was not released until close to the start of the camp week. In addition, staff were responsible for filling out the lengthy attendance form. In 2015, the camp dates were released during informational sessions in advance. Foster parents began completing the camp form with approval from DCF staff, resulting in higher attendance.

Developed by Jacqueline Ford, Program Lead

DCF Region, Facility, and Division Strategies

Solnit Center Treatment Teams

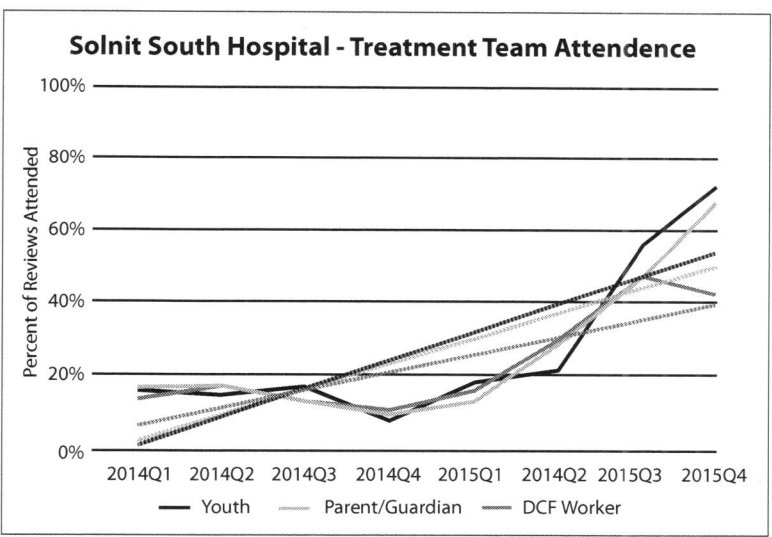

Solnit South Hospital - Treatment Team Attendence

Story behind the baseline:

The significant increase in youth and parent participation is due to a commitment to scheduling meetings at times that were best for families instead of meeting times that were best for hospital staff.

Information developed by Denise Wyrick, Assistant Superintendent

Careline Implementation of the Supervision Model

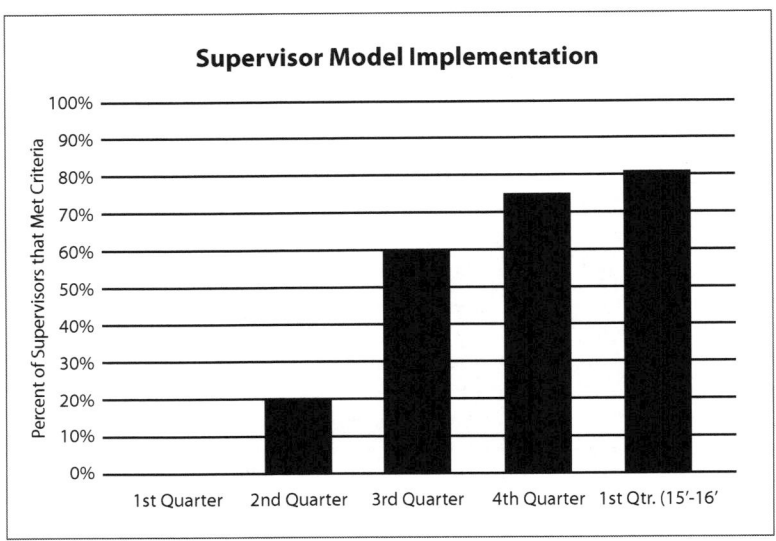

Supervisor Model Implementation

Story behind the baseline:

In 2015 DCF introduced a new supervision model across the agency. Careline managers modeled the correct way to hold supervision meetings for the division's supervisors, assured supervision sessions with staff were scheduled regularly, and then followed up with regular reviews of supervisory notes. By ensuring a strong and consistent process, assuring that supervisors understood what was expected, and then holding them accountable, Careline was able to make significant strides with implementation.

Developed by Dakibu Muley, Careline Director.

Region 5 Reduction of the Number of Children with "Other Planned Permanent Living Arrangement" Designation

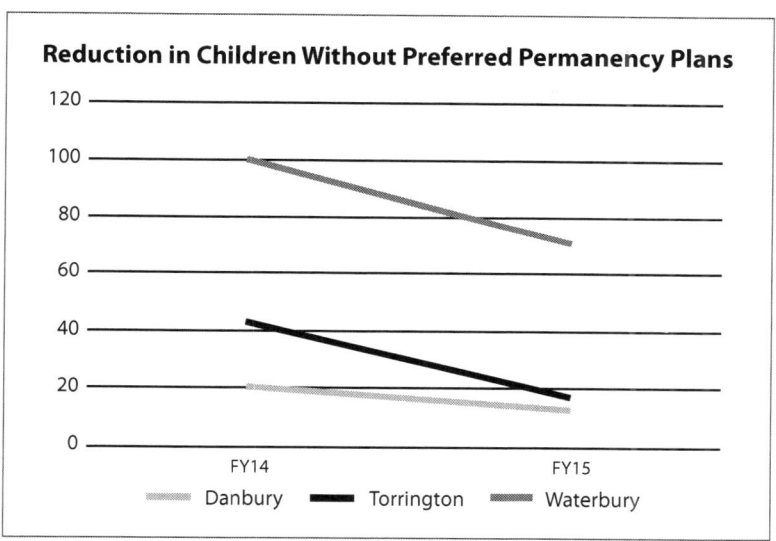

Story behind the baseline:

Preferred permanency for children in care includes reunification, transfer of guardianship, and adoption. The Torrington Office has had a disproportionally high number of children without preferred permanency plans, and has added permanency and behavioral health specialists to case review meetings. Members leave the meeting with specific follow-up tasks. This is significantly reducing the number of children without preferred permanency plans. The two other offices are also using effective practices to decrease the number of children without preferred permanency plans.

Information developed by Lisa Sexton, Program Manager

Region 4 Reduction of Children in Placement

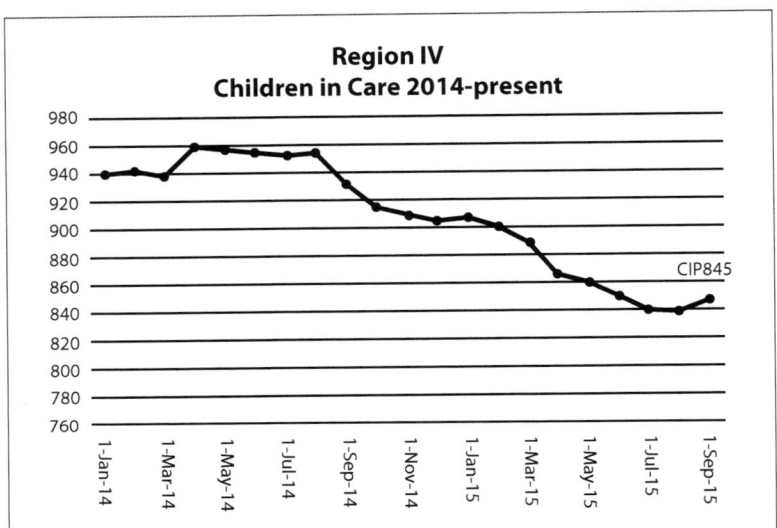

Story Behind the Baseline:

This trend is due to a philosophical belief that children belong at home when it is safe and appropriate. That belief has caused Region 4 staff to remain focused on the Considered Removal Process. This process engages families and their supports (prior to removal) in mitigating safety factors, developing safety plans to prevent entry into care, and utilizing in-home services that support parents with substance abuse issues.

Information developed by Natalia Liriano and Treena

Mazzotta, Quality Improvement Managers

DCF Statewide Strategies

Statewide Considered Removal Teamings

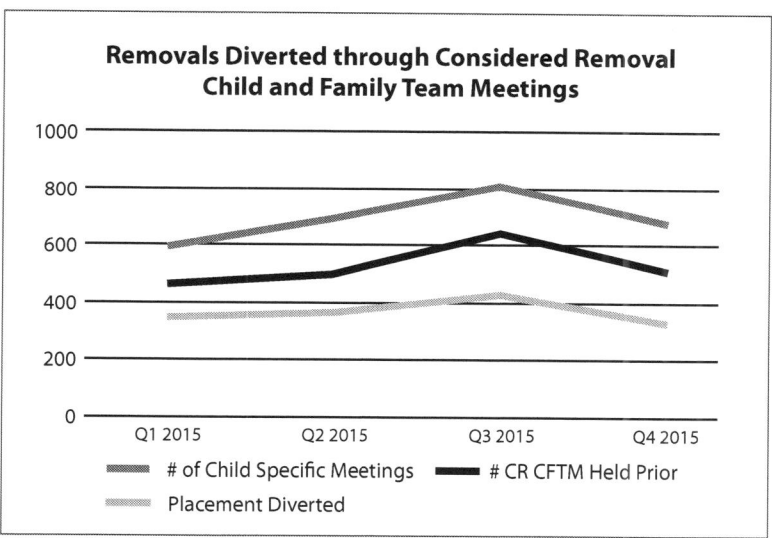

Removals Diverted through Considered Removal Child and Family Team Meetings

Legend:
▬ # of Child Specific Meetings ▬ # CR CFTM Held Prior
▬ Placement Diverted

Story Behind the Baseline:

These meetings bring Department staff together with care-givers and their supports to develop safety plans to prevent entry into care, and to identify in-home services. Most of these meetings are held prior to removal, allowing diversion of 69% of removals. Of those that are recommended for removal due to safety reasons, 71% are placed with relatives and kin, and another 27% are placed with foster families.

Information developed by Kim Nilson, Program Director using LINK reports

Children Placed in Relative Foster Care

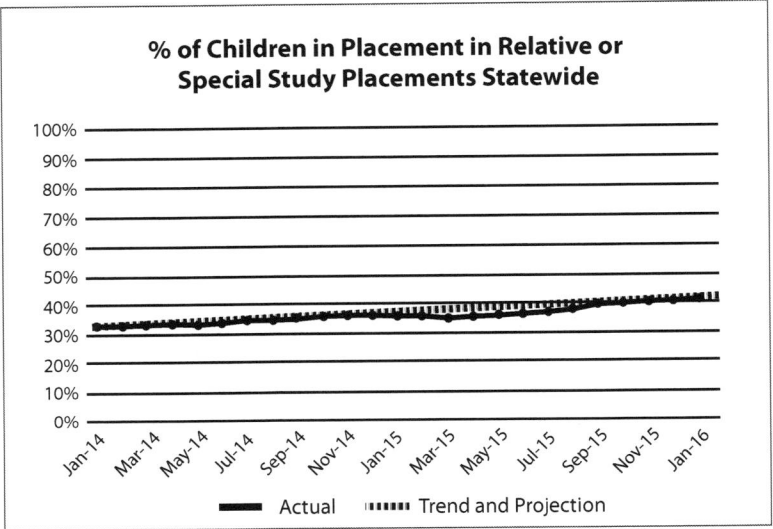

% of Children in Placement in Relative or Special Study Placements Statewide

Story Behind the Baseline:

This steady increase in children in placement who are placed with their own relatives is reflective of Commissioner Katz's commitment to not only reducing the number of children in congregate care, but working with families as partners. The slow and steady increase in children placed with kin is a good example of "change happening in baby steps"; and the ability to increase the number of children placed with kin relies on the effectiveness of programs highlighted earlier in this document.

Data provided by: Bekah Rupert, Public Policy Intern using LINK reports

Children Placed in Congregate Care

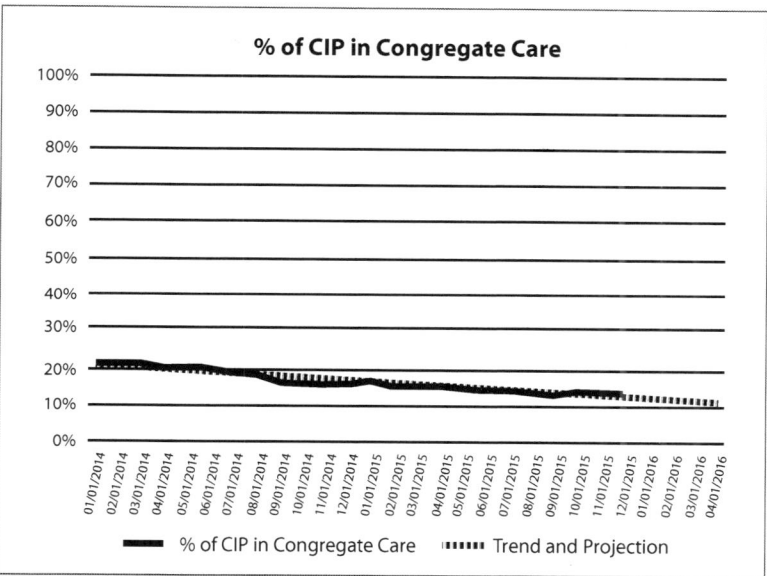

Story Behind the Baseline:

This trend reflects the agency's focus on keeping children with their families whenever safe and appropriate, and when children must be removed, placing them with relatives or core foster families whenever possible. This graph is reflective of the most recent phase of a multiple year effort that has drastically reduced the number of children in care, and the percent of those children in congregate care. The children currently in congregate care have a high level of need, and therefore require continued creative and effective approaches to serve them in the community.

Data provided by: Bekah Rupert, Public Policy Intern using LINK reports.

Made in the USA
Columbia, SC
26 October 2017